ISBN: 979-8860875937

SHORT BASKETBALL STORIES

A COLLECTION OF INSPIRATIONAL, MOTIVATIONAL AND UPLIFTING STORIES BASED ON REAL PLAYERS

JAKE ROW

CHAMELEON
PUBLICATIONS

Hey there, young players!

Get ready to uncover the secrets of your favorite basketball players. Discover the struggles and adversity they had to overcome to become the legends they are today.

But before we dive into these exciting stories, here's something important to remember. While the stories inside this book are based on real players, the adventures, characters and events are work of fiction.

I wanted to give you the experience of understanding the struggles and obstacles these players had to overcome, while creating a story you will remember for a lifetime.

With that being said, you will find a quote from each player linked with their story. These quotes are 100% real.

Will you recognize all of them?

CONTENTS

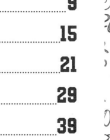

A MOMENT OF GLORY

"I want to be a role model on and off the court. It's something that I take really seriously because I know, growing up, I didn't really have that."

-Giannis Antetokounmpo

The screams of the onlookers made Giannis shudder for a moment. There were only a few seconds left until the end of the game. Now, it was all or nothing. Maybe it wasn't the best idea. Perhaps he should have been more focused. But his eyes searched the crowd raging around him. The coaches shouted, and the other players bumped into him. As he moved across the field with the ball, his eyes continued to search. She had promised to come. She wanted to be there. He just managed to dodge one of those opponents when he saw her. His mother stood in the front row, hands over her lips as she appeared to be praying quietly. She had tears in her eyes as her whole body stood tense among the screaming and cursing people. She was a calm, tense stone in the raging water.

Then, the first tears rolled down her cheeks, and Giannis felt transported back to that time again. He was only 15 when he heard her cry. Crying had become more and more frequent in the last few weeks. Every day she opened letters and read them, she cried more.

Dad left them both a long time ago. He had left nothing behind but debt. Mom worked multiple jobs and double shifts to somehow get him through. She did her best, but it never seemed to her that it was ever enough. That evening, she sat at the kitchen table and wept. This time, it was more bitter than usual. Gianni came out of his room and took her in his arms. Immediately, she jumped up and wiped the tears from the car, giving him a kiss on the forehead, for which he had to bend down to her. "Do you want to eat something?" she asked and already opened the fridge to see what she could do for him. The refrigerator was almost empty. There wasn't much in it except some cheese and sausage. Gianni couldn't remember the last time he saw her eat something.

"It's okay, Mom," he said, but she took the last slices of bread and started making him a sandwich. Gianni knew she was doing this to distract herself. She wanted to direct her thoughts to something that she could fully control. When she cut the sandwich into triangles, she put the plate in front of him, kissed him on the forehead, and left the room.

It was just unfair, Gianni thought. It was unfair that he couldn't do anything. It was unfair that he couldn't help her. She did everything for him. Worked so hard to give him a good life. But he could do nothing for her. Frustrated until he got into the sandwich. The bread tasted old and a bit moldy. But he didn't dare throw it away. It would just be a waste.

Chewing his bread grimly, he looked down at the letters. So many red numbers. As many balances in minus. How long should this go on? What could he do? He carefully began to arrange the letters and place them in a pile. A basketball newspaper appeared under the letters. She had subscribed to this for him, so he had something to do. It was money they needed elsewhere. Gianni decided to tell her to cancel the subscription.

Grumpily, he leafed through the pages and let his eyes wander over interviews and photos. He saw all the basketball stars with their big cars and gigantic houses. He wanted something like that one day for himself and his mother. Gianni was just imagining how he was living in a villa with his mom when the doorbell rang. His friend asked if he would come to the basketball court. Gianni informed his mother and left the small apartment. He and his friends were playing basketball in the park, which drew some spectators to watch. Giannis liked that. He was pleased that people were interested in their game. When it got dark, and he was in bed, he flipped through the magazines again and thought.

Fascinated by the rippling muscles and radiant smiles of the athlete gods immortalized on the two-dimensional paper canvas, Giannis sought more than just idle entertainment in those glossy pages. He wanted to find the solution to the problem. He was so sure it was between the pages of the magazine. And he shouldn't be wrong. These magazines weren't just a pastime. They were his window to a dream of playing basketball professionally and living the life of a sports titan. But not because it was about money or success. No. He wanted to help his mother.

As he turned the pages, he caught the somber refrain of distant sobs permeating through the silence. His mother. He dropped the magazine and pursued the distressing echo to its source - the kitchen. On approaching, a hasty swipe wiped away the remaining evidence of her sorrow. She presented him with a brave smile, one that had weathered storms and braved tempests. Avoiding his concerned glance, she walked into her bedroom. And that's when Gianni decided, he'd become a successful basketball player..

At that moment, he made an unwavering promise to himself. His dedication to the sport took a new direction. He wouldn't just mimic the moves of his role models on a tattered basketball court. He would transcend from shadowing to leading. Every dribble, every shot, every rebound would be more than a game; it would be his ambition, his hope.

He started practicing rigorously, pushing himself further with each day. He joined the local high school basketball team and soon stood out with his resilience and unwavering spirit. His performance didn't just echo in the school corridors but reached the radar of NBA scouts.

Gianni has to grin at the thought. He had been so excited back then. He was so scared. But she had been with him. He quickly dodges an opponent and looks at his mother, who claps uncertainly and doesn't take her eyes off him. She had always stood by him. Was his biggest fan.

For a short moment his eyes look critically at his teammates. Despite his raw abilities, they saw promise, an uncarved diamond, its true worth hidden beneath layers of unpolished skills. They decided to take a risk, nurture this young talent, and give it a fighting chance. Giannis was engulfed in a wave of exhilaration; the glossy magazine prints had finally transcended his reality.

He had fought. Trained. Given everything, And then he had lost almost everything. Just before his first championship game, a knee injury threatened to shatter his dreams.

But he didn't let that get him down. Giannis briefly takes his eyes off his mother and looks at the basket. Just a few more points, and you would win. This throw had to sit.

He saw his teammates nervously looking around out of the corner of his eye. They were all worried about his knee. They all knew the stakes were high. Gianni paused briefly, took a deep breath, lengthened the weight, and jumped.

They all held their breath as the ball flew. All eyes rested on Gianni and the basket. The ball flew. And flew and flew.

As he hit his target, Gianni's ears started ringing from all the yelling and yelling. He saw his mother jumping up and down happily. She clapped and screamed with the other fans.

And then Gianni knew he had finally made it. The scoreboard blinked with the Bucks' first NBA title in 50 years and, above them all, Giannis' shining moment of glory. Gone were the moments when he had to worry about where his mother was getting food from. Gone were the days of modest homes in bad neighborhoods. He had done it. His persistence has paid off. He would never have to worry again. Not only did he give his team a win, he also proved beyond a doubt what a good player he is.

Gianni slowly walked over to his mother and let her hug him. She showered him with kisses while his teammates slapped him on the shoulder.

"You did it, baby," she said, stroking his sweaty face. "I'm so proud of you!" And that was all Gianni needed to hear.

A BEACON
OF HOPE

In the heart of Boston, on a chilly winter night, Dwayne's mother, a frail woman with hardworking hands and a spirit forged from steel, staggered through the front door. She had just returned from another grueling night shift at the local diner, her weary eyes tracing the faces of her six children scattered around the room, the glow from a televised basketball game painting their expressions with a surreal blend of illusion and reality.

Dwayne, her eldest, was transfixed on the game, his promising physique mirroring the very figures dribbling the ball on the screen. Relinquishing a sigh of relief, their mother collapsed next to Dwayne on their worn-out couch, her fingers trembling as she picked up the pile of neglected bills from the rickety table. The letters, emblazoned with overdue stamps and threatening tones, seemed to scream her failure, her inability to provide for her children. She had long since come to terms with the fact that she couldn't change anything about the situation. She was the only one working in the family. And she relied on Dwayne to take care of his siblings when she was trying to make money.

Dwayne, peeking from the corner of his eye, watched as his mother flipped through bill after bill. The tighter her lips pressed, the heavier the silence became. "Why is life so unfair?" he wondered as he contrastively observed the millionaire athletes on the TV and his struggling mother on the couch. He was jealous and envious. He had to admit that. He didn't understand how it could be that some had so much and others so little. The weight of the hammering truth commanded him to change things, to challenge fate for his family.

Summoning every drop of courage, Dwayne turned to his mother, his voice echoing his resolution. "Mom, I'm going to become a professional basketball player," Dwayne declared, his voice raw with determination and an underlying fear.

His mother, though fatigued and weighed by her worries, cast him a gentle smile. This woman, who had hardened against the unyielding cruelty of life, had never challenged her children's dreams, always rekindling their sparks of hope. "If you believe it and you work hard, it will happen. And I will be here to support you any way I can," she reassured, her face softening with the fond faith only a mother could have. Dwayne had thought about it for a long time. He had been afraid to tell her about his plan. It had cost him a lot of courage to reveal his plan to her. But now that she wasn't laughing at him, not ridiculing him, he knew he could do it. She would help him, and he would reach his goal. When the time came, he would support the whole family, and his mother and siblings would no longer live in poverty.

Over the following years, Dwayne's declaration became his sacred contract. With every dribble, he remembered his mother's struggle. With every shot, he saw the overdue bills. Each slam dunk reminded him of his promise, and every chant from the crowd only echoed his mother's words of encouragement.

Though the journey was arduous, Dwayne didn't waver, didn't slow his pace. He lived through cold nights in derelict gyms and sweltering summer morning practices. And with him, through every step, was his mother - standing in the freezing winters to cheer him on school matches, fueling him with meals scraped from bare cupboards, sharing in every joy, every setback. She was on his side. Steady. Loyal. And even if he suffered from one or the other defeat, her support kept him going.

In a neighborhood where dreams often met reality with a harsh chime, Dwayne knew his journey to ketosis was far from simple. With dreams of the court in his heart and adrenaline pulsating through his veins, he roamed the streets in hopes of a basketball team that would foster his raw talent. After seemingly endless hours of persistence and undue hope, he discovered a team that would seal the testament of his fate – but at a steep cost of $30 a month. The austere reality weighed heavily on Dwayne, but his determination didn't falter.

Staring at the night sky mindlessly while lying on his worn-out bed, Dwayne molded a plan in his ingenious mind. He remembered how his friends always admired his skills with a pair of scissors, the sharp blades dancing gracefully through locks of hair. Surely, his barbershop talent could be transformed into liquid currency! At $3 a pop, he could grasp the nettle.

The next day, Dwayne established his makeshift barbershop in his mother's tiny basement. His friends poured in, their heads becoming his canvases. He sheared, trimmed, and shaped each snip of his scissors, bringing him closer to his basketball dream. A symphony of hair falling and clippers humming echoed and filled the room, ample proof that his hands were working magic.

As Dwayne gathered enough for the monthly fee, he joined the basketball team. Wearing a tattered jersey and holed shoes that bore silent testimony to his story, he hit the neon-lit court. Despite his underprivileged state, he outclassed others with his sheer talent and fervor. With relentless practice, he sharpened his dribbles, perfected his passes, and became a pro at shooting hoops.

Dwayne's rise through underhanded poverty to the star player was swift and staggering. His ragtag attire was overshadowed by his determination, tenacity, and raw talent, making him an unforgettable sight in each game. The basketball court became a stage where he displayed his prowess, his threadbare reality lost in the backdrop of his extraordinary skills and an unbeaten spirit.

News of Dwayne's captivating performances was swept up in the winds of acclaim and reached the high halls of the NBA. Sensing the mettle in his vibrato, they saw in Dwayne not an impoverished young man desperate for an opportunity but a triumphant warrior equipped with an undying spirit of resilience. Without a second thought, they offered him a staggering $2.6 million contract.

As the numbers of the offer bounced around his sparse room, Dwayne felt a profound sense of relief knotting in his stomach. As a single word raced through his mind, his eyes swelled up. Mom. The sigh that escaped his lips carried the hope of a future where his mother would never have to worry about unpaid bills. And that he was also able to help his siblings to have a better life.

While Dwayne's journey was defined by hardship and despair, it ended up being an inspiring tale of hope, resilience, and the undeniable power of dreams. It is a testament that sometimes, the most unlikely heroes emerge from the most unfavorable circumstances. In Dwayne's case, they come with a skill in hairstyling, holes in their shoes, and a shining sense of unstoppable triumph. With grit and heart, the dream that seemed too far, too high, finally transformed into reality. Dwayne, the kid from a poor Boston neighborhood, became a professional basketball player, earning not just riches and fame but fulfilling the profound promise he'd made to his mother. And proudly at his side was his unwavering supporter - the frail woman with hardworking hands and the spirit of steel. Her smile, as authentic as the first one when he revealed his dream, was proof that belief, persistence, and love could break the walls of adversity.

In the end, Dwayne, the boy from Boston, didn't just become a basketball player; he became a testament to resilience, a beacon of hope for many more who watched the game from dilapidated houses, reminding them that dreams, no matter how gigantic, with the right mix of belief and hard work, could be as tangible as a basketball in one's hand.

BEYOND THE BUZZER

"Obstacles are opportunities in disguise. Embrace the challenges that come your way, for they are the stepping stones to success."

-Lance Allred

Nine-year-old Lance's heart raced with excitement as he stepped into his grandpa's house for his annual visit. There was something magical about his grandpa's place - it had so many memories and secrets waiting to be discovered.

One sunny day, Lance stumbled upon a dusty old magazine in the attic. It was filled with pictures of towering athletes, dribbling basketballs with fierce determination. Lance's eyes lit up as he flipped through the pages, captivated by the thrilling world of basketball.

Lance was so excited to have found something that caught his interest. "Grandpa," he exclaimed, "What's this?"

Grandpa chuckled warmly. "Ah, that's my old basketball magazine, Lance. I used to watch basketball games a lot back in the day."

Lance's heart raced as he flipped through the pages, soaking in every detail. "I want to be a basketball player just like them!" he announced with newfound determination.

"Ah, basketball," his grandpa said. "It's a game of determination and teamwork. You know, you could definitely be a basketball player too if you put your heart into it."

A few days later, Lance rushed home to tell his mom about his newfound dream.

"Hey, Mom! Look what I found!" Lance exclaimed, rushing upstairs, magazine in hand. He turned to his mom, his voice brimming with excitement, "I want to be a basketball player just like these guys!"

His mom, a warm smile on her face, looked at him. "You really like basketball, huh?"

Lance nodded enthusiastically. "Yeah, Mom! I love basketball!"

His mom's expression turned thoughtful. "You know, Lance, it might be a bit challenging because of your hearing, but that doesn't mean you can't try. Remember, you can do anything you set your mind to."

"Yes Mom!" Lance replied.

His mom, with her hand resting on his shoulder, said, "That's an amazing dream to have. You know mommy will always support you."

A few days later, Lance's mom surprised him with a shiny new basketball. He was very happy and the weight of the ball in his hands felt like potential, like dreams about to come true.

But Lance as he bounced the ball, he started to have doubts. "But Mom, what if I can't? What if my hearing problem stops me?"

His mom knelt down and looked into his eyes. "Lance, there will always be challenges, but it's how we face them that matters. Have fun with your basketball."

Holding the ball in his hands, Lance now felt a rush of determination. "Thanks, Mom!" he beamed.

His mom pulled him close in a hug. "Lance, I want you to always know that you can achieve anything you set your mind to. Don't let anyone tell you otherwise."

Lance nodded, clutching the basketball close to his chest. He dribbled it around the yard, feeling the smooth texture against his fingertips. His dreams felt tangible, almost within reach.

Lance's new basketball quickly became his closest companion. He dribbled, shot, and practiced tirelessly in the driveway. But there were moments when doubt crept in, echoing the doubts he had about his hearing.

One evening, Lance confided in his mom. "Mom, I really want to play basketball, but I won't be able to hear my teammates or the coach on the court. Maybe I should give up."

His mom hugged him tightly. "Lance, you're unique, and you have your own way of doing things. Don't give up because of challenges. We'll find a way."

As the years passed, Lance's love for basketball grew stronger. He spent hours practicing dribbles, layups, and shooting hoops in his backyard. He might not hear the swoosh of the net, but he felt it in his heart every time the ball went through.

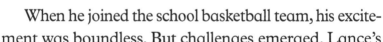

When he joined the school basketball team, his excitement was boundless. But challenges emerged. Lance's hearing impairment made communication difficult.

Lance struggled to keep up. He couldn't hear his teammates calling his name, and his inability to detect approaching footsteps made him an easy target for opponents. It felt like he was out of sync with everyone else. These often led to misunderstandings on the court.

So despite his best efforts, he often found himself on the bench. "You're a great player, Lance, but it's hard for you to communicate with the team," a teammate tried to explain to him.

Sitting on the bench, Lance's heart sank. Doubts clouded his mind. He questioned whether he could really be a basketball player, whether he could overcome this obstacle.

Night after night, Lance lay in bed, wrestling with doubt and frustration. "Can I really become a basketball player?" he wondered aloud, tears welling in his eyes.

But Lance wasn't one to back down. He remembered his mom's words and his grandpa's encouragement. He began to plan his own strategies, training his head to move constantly, compensating for his hearing disability. He developed a sharp sense of reading his teammates' movements and anticipating their plays.

"I can't hear the footsteps of the opponents approaching me," he thought, "but I can feel their energy. I can see their intentions in their eyes."

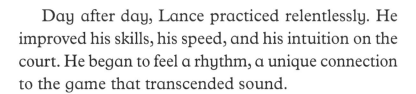

Day after day, Lance practiced relentlessly. He improved his skills, his speed, and his intuition on the court. He began to feel a rhythm, a unique connection to the game that transcended sound.

As the school basketball season progressed, Lance's hard work began to pay off. His teammates noticed his determination and dedication. Coach Richardson, a firm but supportive figure, recognized Lance's potential and began to work closely with him.

One day, as Lance stood on the court, the opportunity he had been waiting for arrived. The coach put him in the game during a crucial moment. He could feel his heart pounding, the anticipation like a drumbeat in his chest.

"You're more than your hearing, Lance," Coach Richardson told him. "You have the heart of a true athlete. Use your other senses to your advantage."

Lance nodded, motivated once again. He went into the basketball court, determined to make his dribbles lightning quick, his passes precise, and his shots unstoppable.

Suddenly, the ball came his way. With a flick of his wrist, he launched it towards the hoop. As it swished through the net, Lance felt a rush of joy. The crowd erupted in cheers, and even though he couldn't hear them, their excitement filled the air.

Slowly, his teammates began to rely on him, not as the "deaf kid," but as an important part of the team.

Weeks later, the day of a bigger game arrived, and the energy in the gymnasium was electric. Lance stood on the court and for the first time, he was in the starting lineup. His heart was pounding with excitement and nerves. He looked around at his teammates, each one a friend who had supported him on this journey.

As the buzzer sounded, Lance's focus sharpened. He dribbled down the court, each movement calculated and deliberate. He stole the ball, made crucial assists, and scored vital points. The ball left his fingertips, soaring through the air in a perfect arc before swishing through the net. The crowd erupted in cheers, his teammates clapping him on the back.

In the final minutes of the game, with the score tied, Lance found himself with the ball once again. His heart raced as he remembered every practice, every sleepless night, and every obstacle he had overcome. With a determined grin, he dribbled towards the hoop, his body moving in harmony with the rhythm of the game.

He jumped, his fingers brushing against the rim as he executed a flawless slam dunk. The crowd's cheers reached a peak, and Lance's heart soared as he landed back on the ground, a triumphant smile on his face.

Lance's journey didn't end there. He continued to work hard, refining his skills and embracing every challenge that came his way. His determination and resilience caught the attention of scouts.

And then, one good day, Lance received a letter - an offer from an NBA team. His heart raced as he read the words. It was a dream come true. Lance Allred, the first legally deaf player in NBA history, was about to step onto the biggest stage of all.

It was a great achievement for anyone, let alone someone who had faced the challenges he did.

In the bright lights of the NBA arena, Lance's hearing impairment was no longer a barrier; it was a proof of his strength and passion. He stood on the court, living his dream, inspiring kids all around the world to overcome obstacles and reach for the stars.

Lance continued to inspire not only with his basketball skills but also by speaking openly about mental health, spreading awareness, and breaking down stigmas.

And as Lance soared through the air, executing one slam dunk after another, a new generation of young basketball players watched in awe, their eyes shining with the belief that anything was possible.

And so every time a ball swished through a net or a crowd erupted in cheers, Lance's spirit was right there, reminding them that anything was possible.

THE
BIG GAME

*"Challenges are opportunities in disguise. Embrace
them, learn from them, and use them to grow stronger."*

-Sean Elliot

In the small, close-knit town of Riverdale, a basketball wasn't just a piece of sports equipment; it was a dream-maker, a friend, a way of life. And for Sean, a bright-eyed young boy, it was his world.

Sean was a basketball superstar—at least in his town of Riverdale. He was 12 years old, with a smile as bright as his future and a passion for the game that made him a legend among his friends. Sean wasn't just part of the Thunderhawks; he was their heart and soul.

Every day after school, you could find Sean at the community court, dribbling the ball with focus, shooting hoops with precision, and laughing with his teammates. His coach often said, "Sean, you're not just playing the game; you're living it!" And it was true. Sean loved basketball more than anything in the world.

His friends would watch him play, amazed at how he could turn a simple game into something magical. "How do you do it, Sean?" they'd ask, their eyes wide with wonder.

"It's not about playing," Sean would answer with a grin. "It's about feeling. When you love the game, really love it, you don't just play; you become part of it."

The Thunderhawks, Sean's team, were gearing up for the championship, and the excitement was building. Everyone in Riverdale was talking about it, but for Sean, it was more than a game. It was a chance to share his love, his passion, his connection with basketball.

The championship game was approaching, and Riverdale was buzzing with excitement. Everywhere you looked, people were wearing Thunderhawks' jerseys and talking about the big game.

Sean felt a mix of excitement and nerves. This wasn't just any game; it was THE game. The one he'd been dreaming of all season. Practice sessions became more intense. Sean and his friends would work on their passes, their defense, and of course, their victory dance.

But then, something strange happened during practice one day. Sean felt a bit out of breath. He shrugged it off, thinking it was just nerves, but deep down, something didn't feel right. He glanced at his coach, who gave him a thumbs up, and Sean pushed through, knowing that he couldn't let his team down.

The championship was approaching, and the town was decorated with banners and streamers. The mayor even declared it Thunderhawks Week! Sean's picture was in the local paper, and his little sister bragged to everyone, "That's my brother!"

But amid all the excitement, that strange feeling kept nagging at Sean. What was it? Was it just game jitters, or something more? He shook off the thought and focused on what mattered most—the game, his team, and making his dream come true. But then suddenly he felt shooting pains in abdomen, it was now clear that there was something wrong with Sean, so when he mentioned this to his mother, she quickly took him to the doctor's office.

Sean's world came crashing down in a cold, sterile doctor's office. The room seemed to spin as the doctor spoke words that didn't make sense: "Kidney disease." "Surgery." "Immediately."

Sean's heart pounded in his chest. "What does that mean?" he stammered, his eyes wide with confusion and fear.

The doctor was kind but firm. "Sean, you have a serious kidney condition. We need to operate as soon as possible. If we don't, it could be life-threatening."

Sean's mind reeled. Surgery? Now? But the game—the championship—he couldn't miss it.

He just couldn't.

His mother's face was pale, her eyes filled with worry. "We'll do whatever it takes, Sean," she said, squeezing his hand.

But Sean's thoughts were elsewhere. The game, his team, his dream—all of it was slipping away. He felt a sharp pain in his chest, but this time it wasn't his kidney; it was his heart, breaking.

That night, Sean lay in his bed, the room dark, his thoughts a swirling storm. The decision weighed on him like a heavy basketball, impossible to shoot.

He thought of his team, how hard they had worked, how much they were counting on him. He thought of the joy of the game, the thrill of the court, the magic that he loved.

And then he thought of the doctor's words, the serious look in his eyes, the urgency of the surgery. He knew what he had to do, but it felt impossible.

He crept to his window, looking out at the basketball court bathed in moonlight. It was calling to him, whispering promises of glory and dreams come true.

"I can't give up," he whispered to himself, tears in his eyes. "I can't let them down."

The decision was painful, like a twist in his gut, but it was made. He would play the game. He wouldn't tell anyone about his kidney disease. He would push through, for his team, for his dream.

He knew it was risky. He knew it was dangerous. But he also knew that sometimes, dreams required sacrifices, courage required pain.

As dawn broke, Sean's face was set, his determination strong. He would play the game, no matter what. He would inspire others, no matter the cost.

The championship was coming, and Sean was ready. But the real game, the game of life, was just beginning, and Sean's courage, his love for basketball, was about to be tested like never before.

Sean's days became a mix of excitement and pain, joy and struggle. The training sessions were harder now, not because of the drills or the opponents but because of the secret he carried and the disease that gnawed at him.

The shortness of breath was no longer a fleeting discomfort; it was a constant companion, a reminder of the battle within. Each jump, each sprint, each shot was an effort, a struggle against his own body.

But Sean didn't quit; he couldn't. His love for the game, his commitment to his team, drove him on. He would wince, grit his teeth, and push through the pain, his face set with determination.

Coach Williams began to notice, his eyes narrowing as he watched Sean on the court. "Are you okay, Sean?" he would ask, concern in his voice.

"I'm fine, Coach," Sean would reply, his voice steady, his eyes not meeting the coach's gaze. But he wasn't fine, and they both knew it.

His teammates, too, started to sense something was wrong. Tim, his best friend, would watch him closely, worry in his eyes. "You're pushing too hard," he'd say, but Sean would shake his head, his mind focused on the goal, the dream, the promise he'd made to himself.

The physical pain was one thing, but the emotional struggle was another battle altogether. Sean felt the weight of his secret, heavy and cold, pressing down on him.

He wanted to tell his friends, to share his fear, his confusion, but he couldn't. He had made a decision, and he had to stick to it. But the silence was hard, the isolation painful.

He would watch his teammates laugh, their faces glowing with excitement and anticipation, and he would feel a pang of longing, a desire to join in, to be free of the burden he carried.

But he knew that he had to be strong, not just for himself but for them. He had to be the Sean they knew, the Sean they relied on, the Sean who could make magic on the court.

His determination was like a fire, burning bright and fierce, but there were moments, quiet moments, when the fear would creep in, dark and cold. What if something went wrong? What if he couldn't do it? What if he let them down?

But he would shake off the doubts, pull himself together, and focus on what mattered—the game, his team, the joy of basketball.

The days ticked by, the championship drawing closer, and Sean's struggle continued, hidden behind a mask of courage and resolve. He knew what he was doing was risky, but he also knew that he had to do it. Sean was ready, his heart strong, his spirit unbreakable. The championship was coming, and nothing, not even a deadly disease, could stand in his way.

———————————●———————————

The day had finally come, the day Sean had been dreaming of, and dreading, all at once. The stadium was packed, the air buzzing with excitement, tension, anticipation. The championship was here, and everything was on the line.

Sean's heart was pounding, not just from the excitement but from the fear, the uncertainty, the knowledge of what he was risking. But he pushed it all aside, focusing on the game, the joy, the love.

The whistle blew, and the game began, a blur of movement, color, and sound. Sean was everywhere, running, jumping, shooting, his body aching but his spirit soaring.

His shortness of breath was more pronounced now, a harsh reminder of the reality he was facing. But he didn't let it stop him; he couldn't. He played with a fire, a determination, a passion that inspired everyone who watched.

His teammates were in awe, their eyes wide as they watched him perform miracles on the court. His coach's face was tight, concern and pride mingling in his eyes.

The game was close, nail-bitingly close, every point a battle, every moment a test. Sean's body screamed in protest, but he didn't listen. He played as if this was his last game, as if everything depended on it.

And perhaps it did.

The final whistle blew, and the stadium erupted in cheers, the Thunderhawks victorious, the championship theirs. Sean's face was a mixture of joy, relief, and exhaustion, his body spent, his heart full.

The locker room was a scene of celebration, laughter, and congratulations. But there was something else in the air, something unspoken, a question in everyone's eyes.

Sean knew it was time. He gathered his teammates, his voice trembling, his eyes bright with emotion.

"I have something to tell you," he said, and the room went silent. "I've been playing with a kidney disease. I need surgery. But I had to play, for you, for us, for the game."

The locker room fell into a hush as Sean's words sank in. Eyes widened, jaws dropped, the silence was deafening, the shock palpable. Then, slowly, his teammates came forward, their faces filled with understanding, support, pride.

"You're a hero, Sean," Tim whispered, tears in his eyes.

"No," Sean replied, his voice strong. "We're all heroes. We played with heart. We played for each other."

His teammates came forward, one by one, hugging Sean, their eyes filled with respect and gratitude. They cheered for him, but it was a cheer unlike any other. It was a cheer for Sean the person, not just Sean the player. It was a cheer for courage, love, and the power of believing in oneself. But amidst the cheers and the heartfelt embraces, there was a sense of gravity, a realization of the journey that lay ahead for Sean.

Days later, in the quiet of the hospital, Sean lay in his bed, his face pale but his eyes resolute. The room was filled with the soft whispers of family, the gentle beeping of machines, the unspoken love that hung in the air.

His brother, always his closest friend and confidant, stood by his side, a smile on his face but concern in his eyes. He reached over, squeezing Sean's hand, a simple gesture that spoke volumes.

"I'm here for you," he whispered, his voice cracking. "I'm giving you my kidney, Sean. We're in this together, just like always."

Sean's eyes filled with tears, not of fear or sadness, but of gratitude, love, appreciation. Sean felt so thankful and loved. It was more than just a brother helping a brother; it was about family and being there for each other.

The surgery went well, and Sean began to feel better. His brother's kindness wasn't just a new chance at life; it was a lesson about caring, sharing, and the special bond between brothers.

As Sean got back to playing basketball, everything seemed a bit different. He wasn't just playing a game; he was living a dream, a dream full of love, courage, and true friendship.

Every time he stepped onto the court, he remembered what he had learned: that being a real hero means playing with your heart, believing in yourself, and never giving up, no matter what. That's what made Sean not just a great player but a great person, too. His story wasn't just about winning a game; it was about winning at life, with the love and support of those who cared about him.

FROM SETBACK
TO COMEBACK

"Your struggles develop your strengths. When you go through hardships and decide not to surrender, that is strength."

-Alonzo Mourning

A team is only as good as its weakest link. That was more than clear to Alonzo. As he sat in the hospital and listened to his doctor utter endless litanies to explain his diagnosis.

It was actually easy to explain. His kidneys gradually scar and eventually become unable to filter blood. What he needed was a kidney transplant.

"Are you alright?"

Alonzo lifted his head and looked at his manager, who sighed and rubbed his face with his hand. "That's the end of the season," Zo finally grumbled, looking at the doctor for further advice on how to proceed. He had looked forward to the next games. He always hated it when making decisions was not up to him.

The doctor continued to talk. What chances did he have of being able to play basketball again in the future? What treatment options were available? Zo didn't hear any of this. He just looked down at his hands, which had been holding a ball a few days ago. Now they looked like the huge paws of a bear. Big, broad, dark. What he now saw in front of him had nothing to do with his body. It was a symptom. The conclusion of an illness he could not control.

Alonzo just nodded when the doctor addressed him without understanding what he had asked. He only had one thought. He would never play basketball again. There had only been one player, Sean Elliot, who had returned to the field after a kidney transplant. The chance that he would fully recover was small, if not non-existent. His career was over. And it was not his decision.

"Zo?" His manager put his hand on his shoulder and startled him out of his thoughts. "Everything will be fine."

Alonzo just nodded and let his manager lead him out of the room. If he said so, it would be so.

What followed were countless stays in the hospital. Partly for observation and somewhat because Alonzo was getting sicker and sicker. His kidney made a poor recovery, and the medication had little effect. He was lucky, though.

His first kidney transplant went well. And after just a few months, he returned to training. After the operations, he felt as if he had lost his life. But now, finally back with his team and in training, he thought himself regaining consciousness again. He was back in the game. He would make it. He would get over it all and carry on as before.

And then it all started all over again. Swollen limbs. Headache. Fatigue. Nausea. His body rejected the transplant; the disease had taken the replacement part over and made him suffer again.

Again he was in the hospital and had the doctor explain in complicated terms what had to be done. What he could do.

Alonzo couldn't take it. He couldn't stand the reporters sneaking into the hospital to secretly take pictures of him. He couldn't stand the questions that were being shouted at him. The force with which people tried to see the big picture. The discussions strangers had about his future. What did they know? Nothing. It was his future! His decision!

He had always been the second man. Always behind Shaq. Always in his shadow. Why couldn't they leave him alone this time?

It was a quiet day when his phone rang, and he heard a voice he hadn't heard in a long time.

"Hey, Zo, what's up?" asked his cousin, whom he hadn't seen for a long time. They last spoke a few years ago. "Why are you calling?" Zo asked, almost growling. Did his cousin now want to enjoy his misery as well? Like everyone else? Did he want to know how he was doing so he could bet on him with his friends?

"I don't know exactly how transplants and stuff have to go down, but I can get tested if you want," his cousin said, and Alonzo paused.

Was this the glimmer of hope he had been waiting for? His last chance?

"You don't mean that," he said, and his cousin laughed. "Why not? You are family. Should I just let you die? You have plans, no? Stuff to do. Places to be."

Zo just sighed. "This is too much," he said and was about to hang up when his cousin sighed.

"Zo, bro, remember when we used to play together as kids? I still remember exactly how much you came to life on the field. I still remember how happy you were when you signed your contract with the Hornets. You fought so hard. Let me help you. It's not over yet," he said calmly, and Alonzo listened.

"OK. If the doc gives the green light, we'll do it!" he murmured.

They ended the conversation shortly after, and Alonzo remained in his living room. He didn't dare to have hope. He dared not count on this transplant to succeed.

They met at the clinic weeks later, and his cousin was examined. They did tests and examined him inside and out. Alonzo stayed by his side, trying to distract him. Like everyone in his family, his cousin was afraid of needles.

"You pee your pants just by looking at the needles. What will it be like when you're supposed to have an operation?" Alonzo asked, and his cousin just laughed.

"Everything for a good cause," he growled and sighed.

It took a little while for the test results to come back. He was a match. He was healthy. He would survive the operation just fine.

Alonzo and his cousin met again at the clinic; this time, things got serious. He would donate his kidney and give Alonzo a chance for a long and maybe successful career.

They were sitting together in the same hospital room. Both

were in their white surgical shirts. They hadn't eaten anything in 12 hours, just drank some water. They were both nervous. Alonzo did not know how to help his cousin. How to take away the fear he felt himself.

The door opened, and the two surgical teams entered. One for his cousin, the other for Alonzo. It would be quick. Precise. They didn't have to worry.

Alonzo lay down on his bed, pulled the blanket over his chest, and looked at his cousin, who had to let the doctor shine a light on his eyes again.

"How can I pay you back?" Alonzo asked, and his cousin just looked at him in surprise.

"Why would you pay me back?" his cousin asked, and Alonzo sighed. Nothing in life came for free. If it wasn't money, then it was hard work that a person had to pay in order to reach significant goals.

"Hey, Zo," his cousin growled as he was pushed away. "If everything goes the way I want it to, you get a win of the season," he said, disappearing around the corner.

Alonzo just laughed and let himself be pushed into the operating room.

The surgery was a success. Alonzo, like his cousin, recovered well. It was only a short time before he got back to training. He recovered so well that he was bought out once and eventually became a Free Agent for the Heats. He was free to choose. And he did.

In 2005, he returned to the Heats, again Shaq's second man. It was the last game of the season when he saw him in the crowd. His cousin. He smiled contentedly at Alonzo. Expectant. Demanding.

Alonzo nodded and studied the score. Things weren't looking good for the Heats. There were still a few points missing.

Again he looked at his cousin, who just raised an eyebrow and crossed his arms. He could almost hear his voice. "If everything goes the way I imagine it, you'll get a win of the season."

He hadn't spoken about the operation. Alonzo understood that now. His cousin never doubted that the transplant would be a success. Why should he now doubt that this game would end in victory?

And his cousin was right. It went the way he had imagined.

The Heats took the win of the season. Even if Alonzo was only on the field for a few minutes per game, his effort was crucial. His team got the win. And as the crowd cheered and everyone gathered around Shaq and the other members, Alonzo found his cousin standing contentedly in the crowd, clapping and laughing before their eyes met. They nodded to each other, knowing he was right. The debt was paid.

Alonzo returned again for the next season. Positive. Exited. But the season should be his last. It wasn't the kidney that ended his career; it was his knee. It failed in one game. He suffered multiple healable injuries but would never be the same again. Alonzo decided to end his career at his own discretion. His jersey has been hanging from the ceiling of the stadium since 2009. His number, 33, has never been reassigned since then.

HOOPS AND HOMEWORK

Mitch adored the game. To him, it was more than just a game; it was his lifeline and the one thing that consistently made sense in a chaotic environment. Due to his severe ADHD, concentrating on most tasks was like using his bare hands to try to catch smoke. However, basketball was unique. Hours seemed to pass quickly after he began making baskets.

Mitch was gifted. No, something more magical than talent. People stopped what they were doing to watch while he was on the court. It was no secret that he was one of the school's stars and that he played for his college squad.

Coach Davis called him over following a particularly exciting game.

The coach asked, "Mitch, have you ever thought about playing in the NBA?"

"Who hasn't?" A broad grin spread across Mitch's face as he answered.

"You've got the skills. However, you must transfer to Division 1 in order to get there."

Mitch's grin grew dimmer. The highest level of college basketball was Division 1. And he was aware of what that meant. Better teams, exposure, and possibilities to play in the NBA. There was a catch, though.

"Your grades, Mitch. You are being hindered by them. You must improve your academic performance to compete at Division 1."

It was as if cold water had been drenched all over Mitch. He had terrible grades, largely because he was unable to concentrate. It was difficult to study because of the muck. His mind would wander after five minutes of reading a book or studying his notes.

"Think about it, Mitch. You just have to dig deep. You've got what it takes."

That evening, Mitch discovered himself reading his textbooks as though they were written in a foreign language while seated in his room. How did he want to accomplish this? He made the decision to consult his dad, the one person who always appeared to have the answers.

His father noticed Mitch's brow was wrinkled and inquired, "What's on your mind, son?"

Mitch outlined everything: the opportunity to advance, the academic requirements, and the difficulties.

His father paused for a moment. He eventually stood up after that. ""Go ahead and grab your basketball. Let's get some fresh air."

When his father walked him outside to their backyard basketball court after picking up his son's textbooks, Mitch showed an expression of confusion. But as he moved along, he dribbled the ball carelessly.

His father flipped open a textbook and said, "Start shooting."

The comfortable routine helped Mitch's restless nerves as he started to sink shots.

His father glanced at Mitch's geography book and said, "Okay, what's the capital of France?"

"Paris," Mitch said, letting go of the ball and scoring another basket.

"Correct. Now, how does photosynthesis work?"

While frowning, Mitch was focused. He said, launching another accurate shot, "It's how plants make food using sunlight."

His father continued to read through and said, "Good, good." "Let's move forward."

They started doing this every day. They would return to the court after basketball practice every day, this time with textbooks and notepads in tow. Mitch's father would quiz him on mathematical equations, historical dates, and scientific concepts as he practiced his shots.

And then extraordinary things began to occur. Mitch discovered that he was able to concentrate on the questions in a way he had never been able to before.

Perhaps the adrenaline from the game played a part, or perhaps it was just the fact that his father had discovered a technique to make learning seem less like a job. In any case, Mitch began to understand. The knowledge was being retained.

The dreaded exam week eventually showed up. Mitch entered the examination room, took a seat, and opened the test booklet's first page after taking a big breath. Panic threatened to arrive for a split second. He then discovered a little basketball and a letter that said, "From Dad," when he opened his pencil case.

Mitch grinned as his anxiety subsided. He took up his pencil and began writing.

The miniature basketball served as a memento and a representation of how he and his father had solved an apparently insurmountable issue. Mitch jumped into the questions with a new sense of assurance.

With each response, he mentally practiced making baskets, almost as though the basket and ball were present in the room with him. When the test's timer went off, Mitch put his pencil down with a sentiment he had never experienced before: hope.

Mitch waited for the results for what seemed like an eternity. He resumed his basketball practice and his study sessions with his father during this time. But he found that his mind kept returning to that exam and the phone call he was awaiting. It arrived at last.

On the sofa table, his cell phone buzzed and the word "Coach" appeared on the screen. Mitch paused. The time had come. It was the time when he would learn whether his efforts had been successful or if he needed to develop a backup plan for his life. He responded with a trembling hand.

"Mitch, got your test results," his coach said. Mitch's pulse quickened. I'm happy to say that you passed. Welcome to Division 1."

As he thanked his coach and hung up the phone, Mitch's eyes began to tear up. Then, filled with emotion, he discovered his father working on some wood in the garage.

"I did it, Dad. I passed!" Mitch shouted.

With all the pride a parent could muster, his father laid down his tools, approached, and gave Mitch a hug.

"We did it," his father corrected, grinning proudly.

Since that time, Mitch has not only excelled in Division 1 basketball but has also improved as a student. He understood that the road to success isn't always a straight one. To get there, you may need to make a few baskets. Furthermore, having someone believe in you can make a huge impact.

Thus, Mitch's life improved as a result of an unusual study strategy and a father who understood his son well enough to guide him. He not only made it to Division 1, but he also overcame his academic difficulties, showing that sometimes the key to getting beyond obstacles is merely coming up with a new approach.

FOUR-FINGERED PHENOM

"All I've been doing is shooting in my driveway and playing 1-on-1 with my rottweiler."

-Gerald Green

Gerald opened his eyes a little at a time. The sterile brightness of hospital lights was the first thing to meet him. He next noticed his mother, who had a look of relief and concern on her face. Her arms tightly wrapped around him as she leaned in for a hug. "Oh, Gerald, I'm so sorry this happened to you," she whispered.

Gerald sensed something was wrong as soon as his senses returned. He turned his attention to his hand, which was completely bandaged. With each wrap he removed, dread creeped in as he carefully unfolded it. He was missing his ring finger.

His mother spoke in a trembling voice as she explained, "Your ring got caught in the hoop." "You had to get here quickly. Your finger had to be removed, so they had to.

It was too much to take in. Gerald experienced a wide variety of emotions, including anger, disappointment, and confusion, but a single thought quickly took priority above all others: basketball. How exactly was he supposed to play that now? He felt a loss for not only his finger but also for what appeared to be his future. His thoughts were racing through each and every shot, pass, and dribble he had ever made. Everything now felt impossible.

It was quiet on the way home. He was lost in his thoughts, and so was his mother. Gerald's gaze became fixated on the basketball hoop in his yard as they pulled into the driveway. It was almost as if it was trying to mock him. He was aware of what needed to be done. He changed quickly, then grabbed his basketball and began shooting. He attempted to, at the very least. Every shot was off, with the ball either going hopelessly wide or hitting the backboard. He continued to shoot till his arms hurt and he lost his composure. He tried everything, but the ball would not go in. Gerald first had a sense of worthlessness and began to doubt his identity and place in the world.

Gerald sat on his porch and looked at the empty driveway as the sun set. His thoughts were in constant conflict with one another. Will he ever be able to play again? What would others say? However, a tiny spark of resolve appeared in him when he went to sleep that night. He would be back on that driveway the next day, shooting his shot no matter what it took since tomorrow was a new day.

The next day, when Gerald woke up, he felt like he had a sense of purpose that he hadn't had since the incident. He got out of bed, laced his shoes, and went to the driveway even though his alarm hadn't sounded yet. From where it lay, his basketball appeared to be taunting him. After taking a deep breath, he grabbed it up and began shooting.

The ball continued to defy entry once more. Gerald, though, was no longer prepared to accept defeat. He continued to shoot, hitting bricks, airballs, and everything in between. His mother viewed from the window, her face a mixture of pride and concern. She was aware of her son's character and understood that this setback wouldn't discourage him.

When Gerald went back to school, the bullying started right away. Along the corridors, phrases like "useless" and "cripple" followed him. Nobody passed him the ball in gym class. They believed he was unable to handle it. Gerald's resolve was only strengthened by everything. For him, basketball was more than simply a game; it was also his refuge and his identity. He also didn't want to give that up.

After doing his homework, he spent hours in the driveway going over everything again because he was unable to rely on classroom practice. Although dribbling seemed strange, he discovered a new method of ball control. It was difficult to pass, but with a different flip of his wrists, he succeeded. The biggest challenge of them all, shooting, called for a completely different strategy. In order to make up for the lost finger, he began using his other fingers more frequently. The ball began to slowly but surely make its way toward the target.

The days eventually grew into weeks, and the weeks eventually into months. Gerald continued his daily schedule of school, homework, and hours spent on that driveway despite the changing of the seasons. His efforts were beginning to bear fruit. He returned to the school's basketball court, but something was different. He had improved significantly. Even his peers were unable to refute what was obvious to everyone else. Gerald had regained his agility and developed a distinctive style, making him a formidable opponent. His setback had become his superpower.

The high school basketball championship finally arrived one day. This was more than just a game to Gerald. It was an opportunity for him to demonstrate that, in addition to recovering from his physical setback, he had actually improved as a result of it. Gerald put the critics to rest with each dribble, pass, and shoot. And as the game's final buzzer sounded, his shot had won it.

Gerald's final shot during the competition became the topic of conversation around the school. He made the game-winning three-pointer with his four-fingered hand, and the footage of him doing so went viral. Newspapers began requesting interviews, and college scouts even started showing up to his games. The same children who had bullied him now aspired to be like him, if not be associated with him.

But basketball was back in his life, now more important than ever, and it was what Gerald cared about most, not his newfound fame or popularity. Even better, he had silenced the voices that told him he couldn't do it, on the outside and the inside. The sweetest win of all was that he had proved them wrong.

One evening, his mother, who had always been his most ardent supporter, sat him down. "You know, Gerald," she said, "life's going to throw at you a lot more than a basketball. It won't always be fair, either. However, do not forget this moment or what you have accomplished. It's proof that adversity can be overcome."

Gerald took her words to heart as he listened. More than just a game, basketball served as a metaphor for his life. If he was adaptable on the court, he was adaptable everywhere. Gerald had this idea and instantly felt unstoppable and prepared to face any difficulties.

After the high school team disbanded around a year later, Gerald was given the opportunity to attend a Division I college on a full basketball scholarship. His mother gave him a framed picture the day he left for college. It was a picture of him making the winning shot in the championship. She said with teary eyes, "Whenever life gets tough, look at this."

Gerald gave his mother a warm hug and tucked the framed picture inside his suitcase before thanking her for her unfailing faith in him. He placed that frame on his desk as soon as he got to his dorm room, which was the first thing he did. It would act as a daily reminder of both the obstacles he had conquered and the possibilities that were open to you when you didn't give up.

From that moment on, Gerald didn't simply play basketball; he lived it, giving the sport his personal touch. And he was aware that every time he stepped onto the court, whether it was for a routine practice or a crucial match, he was carrying something special—a lesson in perseverance, a symbol of the power of the human spirit. Gerald Green, after all, was the man who could shoot hoops with four fingers better than most people could with five. That alone made a huge difference.

MIRACLE
TEAM

"I still can't believe I played on a team that beat the Russians. It's hard for me to talk about. For 20 years now, I've been reliving the moment. I'll be 50 and sitting here, and it'll pop in my head and I'll just start crying."

On their neighborhood basketball court in New York, a group of friends shared the ball, dribbled, and made baskets on a bright afternoon. They considered this floor to be a sacred ground where they could realize their dreams of becoming NBA stars. Jay, Tony, Marcus, and Kevin regularly gathered here after school to practice their skills for hours.

But that week, something was different. Around the age of 60, a strange old man started appearing. He would quietly watch them play every day as he sat on the bench next to them. The friends noticed but at first didn't give it much thought. After all, there were lots of oddball characters in New York.

But after a week of the elderly man's consistent presence, Jay's curiosity won over. He warily walked up to the man. "Hey, sir. I've seen you here a lot. You like basketball?" Jay tried to smile at the elderly man, but he couldn't see his face.

The man stared Jay in the eye and didn't respond. "Spread your legs a bit more when you shoot. You'll score more." The words were weighty and charged as they hung in the air.

Jay froze, unsure of how to react. Was this man crazy? He nervously thanked the elderly man and went back to his friends, relaying the strange advice but laughed it off.

But as the game continued, Jay became aware of how frequently his shots were missing. He suddenly remembered the elderly man's words of advice. Finally, he gave it a try out of sheer desperation. He stretched his legs a little wider before shooting the next time he received the ball. Swish. The puck flew through the goal net. He felt a surge of electricity.

Jay's heart sank as he turned to thank the elder with excitement. The seat was empty. The mysterious stranger had disappeared.

"Whoa, man! Nice shot!" Jay was brought back to reality by Tony's backslap. Jay only nodded as his thoughts were racing. Who was the elderly man? And how did he know what Jay had to do exactly?

The old man reappeared the following day in the same strange manner as the day before. Jay didn't waste any time this time around. He said, "Your advice worked," practically before the man had taken a seat on the bench.

The elderly man grinned and said, "I thought it might." His eyes wrinkled.

Jay introduced the senior while the rest of the team gathered around. They begged him to train them and to impart more of his knowledge. The man thought for a moment and then agreed. "Alright, boys, let's get to work," he announced.

Thus began a chapter in their lives that none of them were expecting and which would change every aspect of their lives forever.

The quartet's game improved to levels they never imagined possible under the guidance of their mysterious new instructor, whom they came to know as instructor Bill. Every day brought a new lesson: court positioning, shooting stances, dribbling tactics, etc. Coach Bill had what seemed like an unlimited amount of advice and exercises, all specifically suited to the boys' unique strengths and shortcomings.

Coach Bill would remark things like, "See, basketball is not just about strength or speed; it's about understanding the game," pausing only to fix his hat or wipe his brow. The boys paid close attention. They had a great deal of respect for him because of the way he spoke and how well he understood the game.

They felt prepared to take on the world, or at least some college teams, after months of intense preparation. Coach Bill set up their participation in regional competitions. The other teams initially didn't take them seriously. a bunch of high school students being led by an unknown old man? It seemed ridiculous.

But as soon as the games started, their mentality changed. The group performed flawlessly as a unit. Marcus was a force on defense, Jay was making three-pointers, Tony was dominating the boards, and Kevin planned plays like a seasoned point guard.

Coach Bill, meanwhile, paced the sideline, yelling directions while also nodding enthusiastically. He was proud, as the boys could tell.

They quickly started to find themselves winning many games. Their reputation had improved. Newspapers began reporting on their winning streak, and before they knew it, they were invited to a charity competition where NBA scouts were reportedly present.

One day after practice, Coach Bill said, eyes gleaming, "A chance to show the big leagues what you're made of." A tension-filled atmosphere of anticipation and nervousness enveloped the room. Everyone realized that this was the chance they had been working so hard for.

The person who had spoken to Coach Bill first, Jay, felt it the most. This wasn't simply a game, either. It was an attempt to prove that hard work and dedication can make dreams come true.

But they were aware that it wouldn't be simple when they stood on the court and observed their opponents during the charity tournament. The opposing teams appeared to be bigger, stronger, and more skilled. Fear started to set in.

Coach Bill then leaned down and said, "Remember, you earned your place here. Now go out there and show them why."

The boys looked at one other and nodded silently. They were prepared.

The charity competition was hectic. As the squad moved through the bracket, it appeared that games were blending into one another. Despite challenges, they managed to go to the finals. Their physical endurance and thinking skills were put to the test. However, they still had one more obstacle to overcome and one more game to win.

The opening period of the championship game was a nightmare. Shots were missed, passes were intercepted, and their defense resembled Swiss cheese. They were down by 12 points when the buzzer for halftime rang.

Their faces were a canvas of frustration and exhaustion as they made their way to the bench. Coach Bill gave them a cold, hard stare, but his eyes were kind. "You're letting the pressure get to you", he said as he began to speak. "Just play, forget about the spectators and NBA scouts. Play as if it were just another court day. You can do this."

There was a silent, thoughtful moment. Jay turned to face Coach Bill after first inspecting his team. "Okay, let's turn this around", he said.

With renewed vigor, they went back to the court. They began to claw their way back, slowly but steadily. Marcus stole the ball, Kevin set up plays that resulted in easy points, Tony made important rebounds. And Jay, well, he was hitting shot after shot like it was nothing.

They were behind one point with only 10 seconds remaining in the game. You could feel the stress. Timeout was called by Coach Bill.

He drew something on the clipboard and remarked, "We've got time for one last play. Jay gets the ball. You know what to do."

Jay stared at their Coach Bill, the elderly man who had turned their dreams into reality as he took on his position. Coach nodded to him. Jay saw an increase in confidence as images from numerous practice sessions flashed before his eyes.

When the ball was inbound, Jay received a pass from Kevin. Five seconds remain. Two seconds were left when Jay dribbled, escaped his defender, and looked at the timer. He leaped and flicked his wrist to release the ball.

As the ball arced in the air and ultimately swished through the net as the buzzer sounded, it appeared as though time had stopped. They had won. Although the crowd cheered loudly, it seemed as though the team was only hearing a faint whisper.

Coach Bill's eyes matched theirs. The silence was appropriate, for words were unnecessary. They had arrived here after a journey that started on a basketball court in their neighborhood. Not as underdogs or a group of immature kids, but as champions, as an unlikely squad, and with an elderly man who found meaning in their dreams.

And somewhere in that group of NBA scouts, notes were written on clipboards. The quartet enjoyed their victory for the time being, but they all understood that this was only the beginning.

RED HAT RIVALRY

Adam had been keeping track of the days, hours, and even minutes left in this basketball contest. Not just any game, but the one with his all-time favorite performer. For a seat near the action, he had cobbled together every penny from his part-time work. He put on his team jersey when the day finally came, gathered his bright red hat for signing, and made his way to the arena in a state of excitement he could not contain.

The atmosphere was overwhelming. The crowd clapped, the announcer's voice boomed over the speakers, and each participant demonstrated athletic prowess that Adam could only hope to match. He watched in admiration as the player he admired moved expertly around the court while executing amazing plays that deserved all of Adam's respect.

Adam's heart began to race more rapidly as his team's victory was announced by the last buzzer. He had the opportunity to meet his idol now. He moved through the crowd waving his bright red hat to get the player's attention while carrying a pen. Their gaze converged as if by fate. His hero approached, took the hat and a pen, and signed it. Adam screamed, "I'm going to play against you one day." His hero raised his head, grinned, and said, "I better get to training then."

Adam experienced a floating sensation that evening. Now that his dream seemed within grasp, he was more inspired than ever. He returned home and continued his training in the makeshift court in his garden. He was on a mission, and the red hat bearing the signature of his idol served as his talisman.

After a few years, Adam had successfully channeled his unquenchable enthusiasm into a lucrative career. He was currently playing in the NBA and was emerging as a rising star. His seven years of sweat, aches, and unrelenting dedication to his profession were finally beginning to pay off.

Although the locker area was bustling with the customary pre-game conversation, Adam was absent minded. This evening was unique. He sat by himself and began to mentally get ready for the game. The gravity of the situation struck him as soon as he got onto the court. He would be competing against his idol, therefore this wasn't just any match.

In the sea of uniforms during warm-up, Adam's gaze automatically focused on one player. He could see the athlete who he had long admired practicing his shots nearby. Adam felt an overwhelming sense of admiration and rivalry.

Adam felt as though the game started in a blur despite the customary fanfare. The applause of the crowd, the coach's instructions, and even the ball appeared to be unrelated variables in this intrapersonal confrontation. Adam responded to every move made by his idol in the first half with a countermove. The first half was a mixture of sideways glances and made shots.

The scores were close to being tied when the time ran out. This victory was crucial for both sides, but for Adam, it meant more than just the scores on the scoreboard. Then, with time running out, he found himself in possession of the ball with his idol guarding him. Then, Adam made his move. He remembered the posture, the hold, and the look his idol had given him years earlier.

He made a slight feint to the left, dribbled to the right, found just enough room, and fired. The ball found its target after soaring into the air. Even though the crowd roared, Adam could only hear the final buzzer. They'd triumphed. While his squad raced, hoisted, and cheered him, Adam's gaze was fixed on his hero, who was already approaching him.

As Adam crossed the court, his heart was racing. It was a mixture of humility and triumph, pitting the satisfaction of winning against respect for an idol.

He finally found himself in front of the guy who had motivated him to make basketball his life's work, but he was at a loss for what to say.

He was about to respond when his idol gave him a knowing smile and added, "I guess I didn't train hard enough."

Adam was in awe. "What?"

"I remember you," his hero continued, "that youngster with the vivid red hat. We are now playing against each other as you promised to do."

Adam could only mutter. Even though he had met innumerable admirers and signed countless autographs, one person still remembered him. Adam cried because of the gravity of the situation. He was only able to utter the word "Thank you."

His hero grinned. "Don't thank me, kid. You accomplished this on your own. You had a dream that you pursued tirelessly. You have a promising future ahead of you."

"Well done, kid," his idol said as they separated and turned around. "I'm going to get in shape so I can beat you the next time," he said, giving Adam a smile that was both congrats and a challenge.

The biggest triumph tonight wasn't only outscoring the opposition, Adam realized as he made his way back to his team while carrying the game ball. It was gaining the respect of a person he had long admired. Not only had he achieved his ambition, but he had also faced it head-on, outwitted it, and even triumphed. The journey was, however, far from over.

The final words of his idol resonated in his ears, igniting his ambition. The following years would be about establishing his worth if the prior years were about reaching this level. There would be more competition, games, and challenges. But for now, Adam cherished this moment where his history and present collided and a wonderful future was hinted at. The teenager wearing the vivid red hat had succeeded, and this was only the beginning.

Adam consequently felt whole as he was surrounded by his colleagues, applauded by the audience, and recognized by his idol. It was a complicated feeling, a combination of joy, relief, and a renewed sense of purpose. Adam realized he had crossed a threshold as he walked away from the court with the cheers still ringing in his ears. He could no longer turn around because he was exactly where he was supposed to be.

SWISH
OF FATE

"Everything I do, I want to be the best. I don't care how you grade me. If I'm not the best, I'm going to find a way to become better."

-Jimmy Butler

As he shuffled out of prison, he could only shake his head. They had grown up together and had done a lot of nonsense together. But Jimmy had never thought that his friend would stray so far. What had happened to him so differently that he had escaped the wheel of hell that had started turning when he was born. He thought about it as he drove his car towards a house.

They grew up in the same neighborhood. Had attended the same school. Was it maybe because he had tried harder in class? His grades have always been slightly better than his friend's. He also didn't have much time to meet friends because his mother worked a lot and depended on him to take care of his sister.

Jimmy was deep in thought as he drove down the interstate. On the side of the road, he saw an old tire rim. That made him smile. For a long time, such a rim had been his best friend.

It was just after he left college. His mother had sat him and his little sister down. In a long monologue, she explained that she couldn't care for them both. That money was tight, and she didn't have enough money to get both children through. That's why he had to go. Because his sister was far too young to take care of herself. Jimmy had felt alienated. He had just started college and only had a small part-time job to earn pocket money. He hadn't even saved enough money to rent an apartment, let alone get a place in a college dorm. And there were no relatives who could help him.

Mom gave him a week to sort out his move. His sister was crying. He was angry. It was a big mess.

Despite the worries about how things should go, he took part in his courses. He didn't show it until the day he was supposed to move out. His friend noticed that something was wrong. Jimmy had a large bag and a small moving box in which he carried his few belongings. His friend Ken asked him what he wanted with all that stuff. Then Jimmy broke down and told him everything. His opposite was horrified. He lived in a shared flat in a small house. They have a vacant room, but he would let Jimmy live there if he helped around the house and helped out with the occasional meal if he could. Relief killed Jimmy. In one go, the problem was solved. He couldn't believe it.

"Jimmy, you're my brother from another mother, dude. You know you're always welcome at my place," he had said, offering a glimmer of hope in Jimmy's bleak world. They had different courses, so Jimmy finished a little later than his friend. Packed with his bag and the small moving box, he trotted down the street, feeling relieved to have a temporary solution to the problem. And yet, he was so tired because he didn't know how things would continue.

As Jimmy continued his dreary path, his attention was stolen by a sight resting in a deserted alleyway: a ragged basketball, abandoned and seemingly forgotten. He picked it up. The neighborhood kids often played here, but Jimmy had never played. Or at least not in a way that you could actually call it playing. Turning his gaze toward the worn-out hoop hanging at the edge of the alley, an impulsive idea commandeered his thoughts. He decided an experimental throw wouldn't hurt if only to divest the melancholy surrounding him.

Jimmy hurled the ball toward the hoop with all the strength he could muster. It whizzed through the air with an untamed momentum, landing straight within the hoop, no bounce, no hesitation, nothing but net. A wave of exhilaration washed over Jimmy, disbelieving as he was. He half-thought it was beginner's luck.

Inexplicably drawn towards the ball, Jimmy decided to bring it along. Perhaps there was an uncharted connection. A sign that he would make the right decision when it came to his future.

Countless streets and countless steps later, he reached Ken's house. Ken welcomed him heartily, offering his place without a second thought. But Jimmy was restless as he eyed the basketball distinctly sitting in the corner of his new room. To him, it was not just a basketball anymore but a beacon lighting the path of his destiny.

They say that when fate closes a door, it opens a window, and perhaps for Jimmy, the window was his newly discovered talent for basketball. It might have started from a need for distraction from his challenging situation, but as fate would have it, the basketball was not just a ball anymore but the key to a door that led to something much more significant.

But that was a discovery for another day. For now, it was home – a friend's house, a random basketball, and the ray of hope kindled by a simple swish of cotton net.

Jimmy sighed at the thought of the first night at Ken's house. Of the insecurity and, at the same time, hope that had been seething in him. They had sat together for a long time and watched a basketball game.

That night, as the flickering glow of a televised basketball game bathed the room, Jimmy watched with wide-eyed amazement. On the screen, men in jerseys danced with an orange ball in an enthralling ballet of agility and strength. The rabid crowd's deafening roars wafted and filled the room with an intoxicating energy. The court was a stage, and each player was an artist performing an incredible spectacle. Jimmy was immediately captivated.

Absorbed in the excitement, ricochet of passes, thunderous dunks, and tides of exhilarating cheers, Jimmy couldn't resist picturing himself among the athletes on the screen. Imagination animated before his eyes, he saw himself clad in regal team colors, dribbling down the court, and flawlessly executing dunk after awe-inspiring dunk. Slowly, it coaxed a genuine smile to unfurl on his troubled face, the first in a bleak and dragging day.

The very next morning, an idea struck Jimmy. Rallying his newfound spirits, he presented the proposition to Ken- to mount a makeshift basketball hoop outside. His request was met with an approving nod. The pair scoured the cluttered garage and pulled out an old, discarded car tire. Work began in earnest, cutting around the thick rubber until it was molded to resemble the rim of a legitimate basketball hoop. Mounted to the weather-beaten wall outside, it was a monument to their resourcefulness and Jimmy's dream.

This simple makeshift hoop became the catalyst for Jimmy's journey. Each day, he would be out in the yard, faithfully practicing under the watchful gaze of the old tire rim. Diligence, combined with innate talent, led him to secure a coveted spot on the college basketball team.

After a splendid college career, he, indeed, became the 30th pick in the pivotal NBA draft. Jimmy was seen as the underdog, the boy from a nondescript town with a humble tire hoop. Knowledge of this supposed disadvantage hung in the air, but rather than suppressing him, it sparked a flame of defiance in Jimmy.

His was a story of embracing constraints. This underdog rode on the surge of indignation and converted it into fuel for his passion - basketball. He danced on the court, painting a performance that left people in awe of his raw talent. Undaunted by celebrated rivals, he kept scaling summits, one game at a time.

With the vigor of an underdog, Jimmy channeled his frustrations into his game, honing it with each passing day. The boy from a no-name town who'd mounted his first basketball hoop from an old tire whirled his way into being an **NBA All-Star.**

The tale of Jimmy is a testament to passion and resilience. His story is etched in the annals of basketball history, a tale of an unassuming boy with starry dreams who rode on the wave of his underdog status to reach the pinnacle of basketball stardom.

From the musty couch in John's living room to the gleaming hardwood of NBA courts, Jimmy's legacy continues to inspire many to re-imagine the impossible, inspiring them to take the leap of faith and chase their dreams no matter how far-flung they might seem.

As the roar of the crowd fills his ears and the flash of cameras blind his eyes, all Jimmy can see is his practice court with a tire rim mounted on a weather-beaten wall. The smiling face of his friend is blazed in memory as he stands on the NBA court, poised as an All-Star, living proof that the underdog can, indeed, have his day.

Jimmy sighed and smiled. Yes, it wasn't all the same, after all, at that time. He had Ken and a basketball hoop made out of an old hoop. Sometimes, it's the little things that make a difference.

DRIBBLING DREAMS

"Success is no accident. It is hard work, perseverance, learning, studying, sacrifice, and most of all, love of what you are doing or learning to do."
-Serge Ibaka

Children's dreams are something innocent. Something wonderful. Every child has this one dream. This one wish is how life should be when the child is grown up. I, too, had such a dream. Many in my life have said that dreams are only for white children. Children from wealthy families with successful parents and a good education at a well-known school. I had listened to this well into my teens. I wasn't a white kid from a wealthy family.

My family comes from the Congo; my parents had hard jobs and did everything to give the children a good life. I was and still am very grateful to them. They taught me hard work and perseverance. They taught me to hold my own in this world.

I can still clearly remember when my parents and I sat at the kitchen table. I must have just turned 18. My dad, always concerned, asked me what plans I had for my adult life.

Something you need to know about me is that I have always loved basketball. Even as a small child, it was the easiest way to find friends like this. Be it middle school, then high school. I didn't grow up in the best area and mainly competed in sports activities. My school performance was also nothing to write home about. That limited my options, as you can imagine. So, the concerns my father had were not unfounded. I had very limited future prospects, and since they wished me to live a full and good life, it was clear that they wanted to know if they could support me in any way.

As a teenager, I was obsessed with basketball. I spent every free minute on the pitch or watched any games. I am a fan of many great players and tried to understand their techniques and to learn some of them. It was apparent then that I would not become a lawyer or CEO of a large company. But I was sure that with my passion and athleticism, I would be successful in basketball.

So, my answer was accordingly. When asked what I wanted to be growing up, I answered, "basketball player." As you can imagine, my dad wasn't really thrilled. He was the quieter of my parents. My mother always spoke the hard words. And this time, too, he gave her a look of help, which made her sigh heavily before she put the cutlery aside and gave me a severe look.

"Papa, Mama," I began, my fork poised above my simple dinner, "I want to be a basketball player." I repeated. . Silence dropped around the dinner table like an anchor. I nervously poked at my food and watched cautiously as my father's brow creased, the muscles in his jaw clenching slightly. He was a quiet, thoughtful man, sparing with his words. His eyes flicked over to my mother.

"But Serge," her voice wavered, "our people..." She faltered, the unsaid words shimmering in the air between us. I knew what she meant. People from Congo do not tread the path of sport, not because they lack talent, but because economic deprivation holds them back. From owning the right shoes to investing in nutritious food for dietary needs, the path is fraught with barriers unaffordable.

But to be honest, the fact has never stopped me. And I couldn't let the argument stand either. Because there were many great athletes in other fields who had made it to the Olympics. Runners, cyclists, and pole jumpers. Why should I be denied the way to basketball?

"Which is why I'm going to Spain. There are basketball teams I can join there," I continued. My reply had brought forth a look of surprise and concern on my parents' faces. But they respected my decision. They knew the worst-case scenario would have me returning home a little bruised but hopefully wiser. No sooner had I voiced the impromptu plan than I realized this was precisely what I had to do. I couldn't let anything hold me back. I would do just that.

The following day, I embarked on my journey.

Spain, a dream sparkling on the horizon, miraged enchanting beauty. Yet, as days turned into excruciatingly long nights, the charade faded. My initial laughter gave way to quiet sobs. I overestimated myself. Spain was absolutely not what I had imagined. I was ill-prepared in my youthful carelessness. Navigating the labyrinth of language, acquainting myself with strangers, and orienting in a terrain unknown, I realized what was harder than what I had bargained for.

Despite feeling akin to an alien drifting in an unknown galaxy, I felt a glimmer of hope when I got accepted into a local basketball team. My heart, soaring momentarily, immediately sunk at the sight of my meager salary. But surviving on sparse resources was my second nature, a skill I'd perfected over years of living in dire straits. My parents weren't rich in my homeland either. I learned how to handle money from my mother at a young age.

My days spun in a whirlwind of training and grinding hardships, of nursing injuries and homesickness. Yet, I persevered. With every dribble of the ball, with every swish in the basket, I witnessed my skills sharpening and strengthening. I saw myself growing as a player, evolving from the boy with grand dreams in Congo to the man inching closer to his goal in Spain. I hadn't thought it would go so quickly. I didn't even expect to be shortlisted. And yet, when the letter arrived one day, a beacon of hope in the mundane - an NBA draft. As I read the lines over and over again, I could hardly believe what I was reading. I was going to be part of the National Basketball Association! I hadn't even noticed that talent scouts were there. Could I have been that focused? Or had it all lost the importance it once had for me? I don't know it. The letter came unexpectedly. When I told my parents the news over the phone, they couldn't believe it. Of course, they called it to the neighbors, friends, and the rest of the family.

The boy who had traveled half a globe with nothing but hope was now wearing the coveted NBA jersey. My first hard-earned paycheck, a magnificent amount, felt heavy in my hands. I was no longer the penny-pinching, struggling athlete. I was a professional basketball player. I now earned so much money that it was enough for me and my parents, who, of course, I took care of. I was in a wonderful position to give back what they gave me all my life. Love and support. If they hadn't allowed me to go the way I thought I would, I wouldn't be where I am today. And I'm more than grateful for that.

Yes, Papa. Yes, Mama. I am a basketball player.

Despite the discomfort it triggered at our dinner table, despite the hardships on my path, that proclamation that night held the power to shape my destiny, to steer me out of poverty and into the world where I belonged, the world of the basketball court.

SCARS AND SWISHES

"I grew up in the projects, and you just didn't have the opportunity to dream. You know, I could have never dreamed of being a Hall of Famer or famous or having the money that I made."

-Allen Iverson

Allen didn't grow up in a good neighborhood. He lived with his teenage mom in the darkest corner of Hampton, Virginia. They were just making ends meet. His father was never in the picture. All were used to the sound of guns and arguments. So it didn't surprise him when he and his mother witnessed a robbery. Whoever thought it was a good idea to open a jewelry store in this area almost deserved it.

He and his mom were walking home when two masked men smashed the window next to them and winced as he and his mom stopped. The gun in his face didn't let him panic. He had quickly learned that it was better if you kept quiet. The burglars told them to shut up and get out of there, or they would find them and kill them.

Allen's mother just nodded and herded him to her run-down house. Here, too, they could hear the neighbors arguing. It was normal for everyone. It was no different at the school. Here, too, there was arguing, fighting, and shouting. It almost seemed to him that his whole world was just loud voices, aggression, and anger. But it didn't bother him because he was safer when he was at home. In the backyard, behind the house, the basketball hoop awaits him. The ball gave him calm and security. He was under his control, and no one could take that away from him. He perfected his moves. Learned to understand the ball like no other. It gave him peace and security. Sometimes, his mother sat in the garden and watched him play. From time to time, friends of his also came along. He enjoyed playing with them.

The older he got, the better he got. At some point, the school team's coach approached him and asked him if he wanted to play with them. He was already tall and just what they needed. Everyone thought better of it. Asked his mother for permission, which, of course, she gave him. And so he became a member of the high school basketball team. Just before he graduated, the coach came up to him and let him know that talent scouts from the NBA would be watching the games.

Allen played basketball at the broken-down, hoop-less court every day until the streetlights came on. His grit was fueled by one overwhelming desire - to make it to the NBA, to be the idol of every child on every court in every neighborhood. Although he did not formulate this wish then, he was firmly convinced that he would achieve this goal sooner or later. It was his chance to get a better life for himself and his mom.

As he carefully re knotted his worn-out laces, his phone vibrated with a call that seemed to resonate every fiber of his being with excitement. It was the coach from his local team, and he bore the news that made Allen's heart race in hyperdrive: THE people from the NBA were coming tomorrow to watch their local league game and see if there was potential in any of their young, hungry players. The coach nonchalantly added, "And believe me, Allen, you're at the top of my list." Allen couldn't believe his ears. Hadn't he done so well in the last few games? The euphoria raced through him like a hot stream.

Elated, Allen rang up his friends to celebrate the news. A wave of emotion seemed to carry them all to a favorite local hangout - an unpretentious bowling alley where one of Allen's friends was playing a competition later that night. They were caught up in the blizzard of elation, echoing alleys filled with loud cheers, cold beer, and a blockbuster celebration. Looking back, Allen isn't sure if staying out for so long was such a good idea. After all, he had an important game ahead of him.

Unfortunately, as the Greek philosopher Heraclitus once remarked, you cannot step in the same river twice. Unbeknownst to Allen, his tide was about to turn. A dismissive shoulder bumped into Allen, staining his favorite jersey with beer.

The man, reeking of alcohol with a stained t-shirt that once was white, glared at Allen as if Allen was the culprit.

Allen apologized, but his sincere remorse fell on deaf ears. Furious, the stranger, probably a local lug with too much alcohol fueling his aggression, Allen shoved. Memories of schoolyard fights flooded back. All the aggression surrounding him during childhood seemed to come at him in one fell swoop. Allen saw the belligerent man taking a potluck swing at him, but he skillfully dodged. Sensing an opportunity, Allen took a lightning swing of his own, flooring the bloke with a single punch. He had always tried to avoid such arguments, but something had taken his restraint that evening. Maybe it was the excitement. The upcoming game. The general stormy mood that had gripped him since the news.

Before he knew it, the flashing blue and red lights of a police car arrested the festive scene. The same man who started the brawl was now slurring a tale of being attacked unprovoked. Officers escorted Allen to the police station where he was held overnight - a night that seemed as long and torturous as a losing game, drenched with regret. Allen was sure that his chances of being discovered by NBA scouts was now non-existent.

The following day, freedom came just in time for the game. Allen ran from the station, hoping the news of his arrest hadn't reached his coach or the NBA scouts. His heart pounded with a violent rhythm, each beat a painful reminder of the night before. The anticipation and fear felt like he was dribbling on the edge of his dream's cliff.

As he stepped onto his home turf – the court, the NBA scouts fixed a stern gaze on him—news travels faster than light in the tightly-knit basketball circles. An apprehensive silence fell on the crowd. His disastrous night seemed to echo in their collective consciousness. Yet Allen stood tall, holding the veneer of his dream steadfastly against his fear.

The game commenced, and Allen played - not just for the scouts but for his dreams, his neighborhood, his coach, and the boy he once was, looking up to the giants of the NBA. Every dribble, every shot seemed to tell his story. His agility, paired with the gritty determination etched across his face, made for a spectacle that not even the harshest NBA critics could dismiss.

His performance spoke louder than the clamor of his infamous night, and the NBA scouts were visibly impressed. After rounds of discussions, they decided to give the young prodigy his dream. Allen was selected as the first overall pick for the 1996 NBA Draft, earning the admiration of his friends and coach and a newfound respect in his neighborhood.

Allen's tumultuous journey was not without blemishes; he knew the world at large would remember his misstep. But that boy who dreamt beneath the hoopless court learned that he was made for greatness, and so he proved, from the playground to the NBA, that dreams can rise above the night's darkness. And it paid off.

He no longer lived in the brutal neighborhood and no longer had to be threatened. He has left the aggression of his homeland behind.

A MOTHER'S GIFT

"Basketball is more than just a game; it's a way of life. It teaches you discipline, teamwork, and the importance of never giving up."

-Olden Polynice

On a crisp spring morning, a hush descended upon the sterilized corridors of St. Mary's Hospital. In a shaded room, the numb silence was broken by the hesitant cooing of a newborn baby, a hauntingly beautiful sound that cradled everyone, and two shaken hearts in particular, into a tender, hopeful vigil. With their somber faces worn with wisdom and age, the doctors reluctantly approached the mother, who had just given birth to her first child, a boy, now nestled lovingly in her arms. His name was Olden, the light of the family yet to unwrap their joys.

"We're sorry…" The voice carried a grief that lingered in the air, feasting on their joy like acid on sunshine. "Your son, Olden… he has a deformity. His feet are turned inwards, which makes independent walking impossible..." The words hung in the air, poisoning the atmosphere with their cruel reality.

The mother's eyes filled with resilient tears, clutching Olden tighter. The beautiful, innocent facial curves of Olden, blind to his existence's most significant hurdle, shook his mother to her core. She looked at her husband Jason, a man who wore his poker face like a defense, but not today, not now; his eyes mirrored his wife's agony. But, there was also a glimmer of hope, the tiniest flicker in the overwhelming darkness.

She searched for answers and pleaded with the doctors, "Please, there must be something we can do."

The doctors, though quite skeptical, introduced the possibility of using specialized leg casts that might correct the deformity. However, they warned her it was a long shot and would require a considerable investment, financially and emotionally. The casts were expensive, and Olden would need to wear them for years.

She nodded, pain and determination etching lines on her brow. "We will do this. I want my baby to walk, run, and live his life ensnared by no chains."

In their quaint tiny home, she juggled her primary and secondary jobs, the sweet whispers of her sleeping Olden the sole sweet symphony fueling her. Her husband became a rock, shouldering their life's burden with a silent agreement that this overgrown hurdle perhaps was silently thriving their unyielding love.

As years passed, Olden grew, his world confined within the custom-made casts, but his spirit was free, eager, and unbridled. They are always found giggling, wooing their old neighbor's cat, or even painting the sun with tranquil shades of blue. But his destination was his mother's lap, where he'd fall asleep listening to stories of heroes, journeys, and indomitable spirits.

One day, after a few years, time was ripe for the casts to come off. The small gathering at St. Mary's Hospital was a blend of familiar faces, their expressions cloudy with faint hope and palpable tension. Olden, the center of everyone's attention, lay on the hospital cot, shrouded in childish curiosity, unaware of his silent fight.

An eternity later, the casts were off. Olden was upright, held by the firm hands of Dr. Sullivan. "Olden," Rebecca whispered, opening her arms wide, "Come to Mama, darling." Her voice shook, and her lips quivered as she pushed through her tears, a beacon of determination. Olden looked at her, his eyes wide with innocence and wonder.

He took one step. He cried, but his eyes were still on his mother. Another step, and then another. Cheers and claps filled the room as Olden, now swaddled in his mother's warm arms, beaming with joy, made the impossible possible. Yes, Olden had finally walked, a captivating spectacle of unyielding love and resilient human spirit. They all cried that day, the tears a crystal symphony, weaving a saga of hope, faith, and the power of a mother's love — the tale of the Miracle of Baby Olden.

40 years later

In the quiet slumber of the pre-dawn morning, Olden awoke to the first tendrils of sunlight sliding over the foot of his bed. With a weary sigh, he pushed off the heavy quilt cover and slid his feet onto the cold wooden floor. Shuffling over to the weathered mirror mounted on the bathroom wall, he squinted his sleepy eyes at the face staring back at him. Wrinkles etched deeply over a once youthful skin, the piercing blue eyes now dimmed and faded, and yet the cheeky boyish grin remained the same.

Walking downstairs, he traced his hand over the countless trophies, awards, and jerseys adorning every inch of the hallway and living room. The room was a shrine, a testament to a glittering career as a legendary basketball player. Silver glinted, and gold shimmered under the spotlight. Framed pictures echoed silent cheers and the sweet taste of victories. The autographed balls bore silent witnesses to the many hands that had shared them, the countless successes, and the seldom defeats.

Olden walked past the intricate webs of memories with an air of reminiscence. There was the trophy from his first regional title, the signed jersey from his debut season. His Shimmering MVP award stood majestically, a beacon that marked the climax of his flourishing career. Each trinket and every photo was a stepping stone on the path of his remarkable journey - a journey from being a kid in the streets to a basketball hero in the hearts of millions.

However, amidst the sporting grandeur, one frame stood more significant than all the glimmers of gold and silver. Right in the middle of everything, encased in a simple wooden frame, was a familiar and loving face - his mother. Below her radiant smile, in delicate cursive, was etched - 'Thank you for giving me the opportunity to walk.'

Olden stood in the golden warmth of morning light, gazing at the picture with misty eyes. His mother had often joked that his legs were longer than his body as a child, constantly tripping over his own feet. Little did she know, those very legs would one day carry him across courts, under the roars of a thousand fans, and into the annals of basketball history.

She had been the pillar in his life, his shooting star. Ever encouraging and eternally motivating, she had believed when no one else did. The countless sacrifices she made for him, the lullabies she sang when he was ill, and the life lessons she taught were what shaped Olden into the man he was. She gave him the chance to walk when the odds were stacked against him. She was his first coach, cheerleader, biggest fan, and mum.

Slowing his breath, Olden placed a trembling hand on the glass of the wooden frame. A serene sense of gratitude washed over him. His victories were only possible because of her faith and investment in him.

Indeed, while trophies gleamed and photos recited tales of joyous wins, none surpassed the importance of that one picture. It symbolized a mother's love, a testament to her belief and sacrifices. Olden looked back at his reflection in the frame's glass - a successful man, a court legend, and a mother's proud son. His smile widened, a chunk of his age-worn heart brimming with a wholesome glow.

MIND
OVER MATTER

"I've been through so much, and there have been a lot of ups and downs. But at the end of the day, the good outweighs the bad. I'm blessed."

-Derrick Rose

Derrick, a prominent figure on the basketball court, found himself in the throes of a fiercely competitive game. The moment was tense, as it is often in the final quarter. A concoction of emotion brewed in the arena - excitement, anticipation, fear. It was all resting on Derrick's broad shoulders. He squared his feet, took aim, and just as he prepared to shoot, a sudden, sharp pain shot up from his knee, which rooted him to the ground.

The world seemed to lurch sideways, and Derrick's vision blurred, tunneling around the edges. A large, disorienting ringing noise filled his ears, drowning out the cacophony of the restless crowd. Colors mixed, and the figures of his teammates and coach seemed ethereal, like a mirage, as they scrambled toward him. The panic rising in him made him shudder. What happened to him? What happened to the game?

The medics and players on the court were a blur of motion, their screams fading into an indecipherable hum. He felt his body being lifted, a sensation of floating, and then everything went black.

Derrick eventually flickered back to consciousness, the sharp smell of antiseptic rousing him from a pitch-black abyss. His surroundings were clinical and cold, sterile whites and blues replacing the familiar view of the pulsating, vibrant court. Lying on a pristine hospital bed, he looked around in confusion until his eyes landed on a familiar, comforting sight.

His girlfriend was there. Relief washed over her face as she hugged him, her chestnut eyes gleaming with unshed tears. In her gentle, mellifluous voice, she unveiled the unfortunate events that led him here.

"You tore your ACL, Derrick." She held his hand, her touch a warm contrast to the pervasive cold of the room. He blinked, taking in the information without really processing it. Torn ACL. Not a twisted ankle or a minor sprain but a torn ACL. A career, possibly on hold.

His heart sank when the doctor strolled in, a somber expression etched on his face. With a clinical tone, he detailed Derrick's situation, weeks of grueling rehab and physiotherapy, and, most disheartening, a sabbatical from the one thing Derrick loved more than life itself – his game.

Turned out, his basketball was not just his strength and passion but also his Achilles heel. The doctor cleared his throat, clipped words hanging in the sterile air. The hard truth rang in Derrick's ears, his hoop dreams vanishing like a lonesome breeze.

Yet, amidst all the chaos and confusion, Derrick found a strange sense of determination. The look in his girlfriend's eyes, the memory of the electrifying game, the roaring crowd - they rebounded in his heart. This setback would be his stepping stone. His quarter may have ended, but his game was far from over. The hospital room's chill began to feel less heavy, a spark igniting in Derrick's eyes. He would fight this. He would rehabilitate, rise like a phoenix, and reclaim his game. The court might be at rest, but the player was awake, ready, and more than willing.

The first twenty-four hours without basketball felt like a torturous eternity. He felt lost, devoid of his defining purpose. His days became gloomy and monotonous with him bound to his wheelchair, his leg a cruel statement of his reality, a painful reminder of his lack of control. He felt his physical health waning as muscle turned to fat and dexterity morphed into awkward clumsiness.

And yet, Derrick did not surrender to despair amidst this dark cloud.

Instead, he began to see this forced hiatus not as a death sentence but as an opportunity to deepen his understanding of the game he loved. Rather than succumbing to incapacitation, Derrick decided to train his mind in the art of basketball.

He immersed himself in studying games, analyzing player strategies, tracing the patterns of interceptions, and dissecting the nuances of record-breaking shots. As he sat immobilized, his mind began to flex and stretch toward new horizons of the game.

In the midst of this mental training, Derrick noticed how the game was more than speed, power, and athleticism. It was like a symphony that required tactful handling of tempo and rhythm, demanding an innate understanding of space, timing, and coordination. He started noticing the subtle signs of approaching offense, the telltale body language of an impending bluff, and the artful ways to confuse opponents.

Nine long months drifted by. Although Derrick missed the adrenaline rush, the sweat, the cheers, the high fives, he grew. His mind had become a treasury of basketball knowledge. The time had come for his leg cast to be removed, a moment he'd eagerly awaited. But he knew he was not the same person anymore. He would have to approach training gradually. His body had to feel its way back to the whole movement.

He hit the court with a healed body and a mind brimming with understanding and strategy. The rust rubbed off quickly. His body remembered the moves — the swift dribbles, the high jumps, and the precision throws — but with renewed vigor and refinement.

Gradually, he started implementing his newfound knowledge on the court. Every fake, every pass, every shot was engineered with precision. Derrick, who used to be known for his raw power, had now become an artist on the court, painting masterstrokes trailblazing his way to victory.

Within a month of training, Derrick found himself at the peak of his talent. It was as if his injury and hiatus had bestowed him with a strange, empowering wisdom that tamed the round ball in truly incredible ways. His rivals were left defenseless against his prowess as he defied all predictions. He had discovered a whole new gift for himself. He wondered if he would have reached that point had he not sustained the injury. However, he could not give himself the answer.

Derrick's name started ringing in every stadium, a testament to his remarkable comeback. He became a story of resilience and intelligence and an icon of the game. His ceaseless will to strive and improve and his ability to adapt and learn birthed a legend on the court.

It was evident now. Derrick had not merely spent his days of recovery idling; he had metamorphosed. He was no longer just a player; he was the game. His days without basketball, rather than driving him away from the game, had brought him closer, making him understand the game's soul better.

Basketball was no more just a passion for Derrick; it had become his life's poetry—beautiful and powerful, challenging and rewarding: a game resonating with the symphony of life itself. And thanks to all this new knowledge, he led his team from victory to victory.

LIMP
TO LEGEND

"Your biggest enemy is yourself. It's what you tell yourself every day that either pushes you to greatness or keeps you in mediocrity."

-Paul George

The wooden arena floor echoed under the thunderous applause of the cheering crowd. Tonight was no ordinary game; it was an event that most college basketball players could only dream of. On the courtside sat the talent scouts of the NBA, with their eyes prying for the next top draft.

Among the young, adrenaline-charged athletes donning their school colors, Paul had the most to offer -- and the most to lose. Having skillfully dominated this season, he embodied an athletic epitome, a beacon of hope for the rest of his team. His heart was as relentless as the crowd's roaring; with each beat, it whispered insistently, 'NBA.' He wanted to make it. He had to make it. Such a change usually comes only once. He had to convince the scouts. Even if that meant that maybe others on his team would shine less.

As the game convened, Paul showed an endless array of skills and commitment. His nimbleness. His jump shots seemed to defy the very law of gravity. But as enchantment so often paves the way for disaster, his dream was about to take an unfortunate detour.

In the midst of a heated face-off, Paul's foot skidded. For a split second, time stood still, and then came the sound that silenced the roaring crowd - a sharp snap, almost like a bone breaking. His body crumpled to the floor, the pain too sheer to disguise. His heart beat a bit faster, off rhythm, off sync as he held his foot in disbelief. His fingers felt his leg and foot. He couldn't feel anything from the outside, even if the pain inside ate through his limbs like lava.

There he was, lying on the ground with the unforgiving pressure of the future bearing down on him, as he realized the shocking reality - his foot was injured, and each tick of the clock was a mocking reminder of his elusive NBA dream.

His eyes scanned the shocked expressions of his classmates, the worry in his coach's eyes, and the concerned but distant grimace of the NBA scouts. He had two choices: surrender to the excruciating pain and walk off the court to salvage what was left of his hurting foot, or exert every ounce of his strength to stand tall and prove his worth to the waiting world outside of his college turf.

For Paul, the thought of relinquishing his dream was not an option. With a defiant spark in his eyes, he lifted himself off the floor, each movement a sting of torturous pain. Unflinching, he gave the referee a thumbs-up single, a testament to his invincible spirit. He would not bow to the pain. He wouldn't let this chance pass him by. He had no choice but to persevere. That was the one moment that would take him further in life. Even an injured foot couldn't change that.

Paul played on each step in agony, yet he ran, jumped, and dunked like a man possessed. The pain burnt through him, of course, vibrant and all-consuming, but strangely, it began to fade in the background, nudged aside by the surge of adrenaline taking over. Courage bestowed him with superhuman strength, numbing his physical agony and sharpening his senses.

As he moved fluidly against his opponents, the crowd watched in awe. He sent balls spinning into hoops, pushed limits, and perhaps even redefined the very definition of the game. As each minute ticked down, Paul shone brighter than he ever had, bearing a newfound torch of resilience.

His agony was his secret, his shattered foot the foundation of a legendary performance. One can almost say he was rising, phoenix-like, out of the ashes of his shattered dream, soaring straight towards the dazzling destiny that awaited him, proving with each agonizing step that he could - and would - overcome anything in pursuit of his NBA dreams.

As the final whistle blew, Paul, driven by cores of pain and passion, clinched the victory for his team. He had weathered the most brutal storm of his life. But despite the intense pain, the victory felt sweet. He was no more a mere college player; he was a warrior who led his army to a glorious win, with the eyes of the NBA witnessing his incandescent saga.

Paul's story is not just one of a broken foot and a fueled determination. It's a tale of a man who chose to face adversity head-on, not as an obstacle, but as a stepping-stone to his dream. He had decided to play that game, to dance with pain, all for the love of his vision. It is a tale of hope and resilience, a young man pushing beyond the breaking point in pursuit of his NBA dreams. And in doing so, he won more than just a game – he won a future. He won a chance to leap into destiny. He was not the biggest player on his team, nor the fastest, yet he was the one with the indomitable will.

A coarse concrete-made city court was the backdrop against which every streak of sweat on Paul's determined face glistened. His heart pounded in sync with each thud of the bouncing ball, and his every step matched the rhythm of the game, making his performance feel less like a sport and more like an enthralling dance number. He painted magic on the court every time he played, and his love for the game was unquestionable.

While he limped, wobbled, and veered, he didn't yield. His game might have faltered, but his spirit didn't. His contributions helped his team to secure a hard-earned victory that day. Once the climax lettered "GAME OVER," flashed on the scoreboard, he finally allowed himself to yield. He made it. The game was over.

Almost painfully, he slowly eased his limping foot off the court and settled on a bench nearby. He mopped his face with a towel and hunched over, trying to soothe the throbbing in his foot. It was then, through the damp corner of his towel, that he saw the man approaching him. He just kept seeing him out of the corner of his eye. He didn't know his name, but he knew he was about to have the most important conversation of his life.

This man was no ordinary spectator; he was a well-known face from the NBA. Paul could barely believe his eyes as he watched this influential figure stride toward him with a pensive expression. The scouts rarely addressed the players directly. They mostly disappeared as unseen as they came, only to make their decisions official days later. But this time, it was supposed to be different. The man crouched in front of Paul and gave him a searching look as if he'd seen through him.

"I saw real determination in you today, son," the man said. Paul, feeling a rush of adrenaline, immediately responded, "Thanks, Sir. I've been practicing." Paul forced himself to be humble. Nobody liked big-headed people. And while his talent on the field was necessary, it was also crucial that the man liked him. because compatibility with the other players was also important.

The man shook his head and corrected him, "I am not talking about your basketball skills. I've seen plenty of players with skill. I'm talking about your unquestionable spirit. I spotted your struggle; you've got a broken foot, haven't you?"

Paul was taken aback. He was forced to admit his disadvantage, revealing the intensity of his pain. Yet the pain seemed momentarily insignificant when he saw the respect in the man's eyes. He nodded slightly and saw out of the corner of his eye how the trainer had already called a doctor. Then, it occurred to him for a moment that all of this could now take revenge. By continuing to play, he might have caused more damage than he initially would have done.

"Courage, true grit, and spirit, these are much more difficult to find than talent," the man said, his voice filled with awe. He pulled out a business card and held it towards Paul. "Call me tomorrow."

And with that, he shook hands with Paul, patted him on the back, and headed towards the field. Still in shock, Paul clutched the card, barely noticing the throbbing in his foot. He had caught the eye of the NBA. The triumph was worth the pain.

His spirit, passion, and courage had invited opportunity to his doorstep. As the pain in his foot came crashing back, he sat there, feeling triumphant, almost forgetting the pain. Happiness coated his every vein.

In the end, he realized that he was always a winner because he was, indeed, bigger than the game. Of course, he was out for a while because of the foot. But that wasn't bad because when he came back, he was signed by the NBA. It was the beginning of his career. It couldn't have been worse. And he proved that, in the end, strength is what matters most. And he had proved that from the start.

AGAINST ALL ODDS

"No matter where you come from or what you've been through, you have the power to change your life. It starts with belief and determination."

-Caron Butler

Caron's eyes fluttered open at 6:30 on a chilly Thursday morning, his alarm clock blaring mercilessly amidst the silence of their cramped, tumbledown home. He stretched, yawning, as the weary sound of all his seven siblings rousing from sleep pervaded the space. He didn't know why his siblings always had to be so loud. It was slowly starting to get on his nerves. But then again, there was nothing he could do about it. It is what it is.

He shuffled downstairs, arrested by the scent of breakfast. His nose wrinkled in immediate disappointment as his gaze fell on the all too familiar sight of beans and toast sitting meekly on the beaten wooden table. His mother was bustling around the kitchen, adding more fuel to their old, stuttering stove.

"Beans and toast, again?" Caron groused, slouching into his chair. His grumble echoed in the noisy morning cacophony of siblings arguing, spoons clattering, and the muffled radio news. But his words managed to reach the only ears they were intended for. He hated beans and toast. He knew it was the quickest, cheapest, and easiest meal she could put on the table with the number of children in the house, but sometimes he wished there was something else.

"Yes, Caron. For the fifth time this week, if I'm not mistaken," his mother's voice sailed across the kitchen, laced with fatigue. She turned to him, wiping her hands on her old, battered apron. Her eyes, vibrant like his own but weathered with worry lines, met his in a silent battle of wills.

"But, I'm tired of beans and toast, Mom!" he protested, his gaze locked with his mother. "Jimmy's mother packs him pancakes and sausages!"

His mother's smile held a tinge of sadness, but her voice never faltered. "Jimmy's mother also doesn't have eight children to feed, love." Her voice was patient yet weary, a phenomenon born from years of soothing hungry bellies and hurt feelings in equal measure. Caron knew what he said next might hurt her. But he was frustrated not only because of the breakfast that just didn't satisfy him but also because of other things that kept him busy. For example, the school he had to go to.

"But we aren't exactly dining fancy, Mom! Beans and toast all week!" Caron stood, his chair scraping against the floor, as his siblings watched the scene unfold. His mother, a constant pillar of strength, simply sighed.

"We aren't living in riches, Caron. We make do with what we have, not what we want," she said, her voice barely above a whisper. She resumed her bustling, her armor of patience seamlessly mended and worn again amidst the pressing onslaught of their poverty.

Caron didn't retort, stomping towards the front door, his backpack slung over his shoulder. The taste of disappointment was better than the cold beans he hadn't touched. The chaotic household's clamor was the harsh symphony that escorted him out into the frosty morning. He knew it was unfair of him. His mother did everything to feed the children in the house. She tried to give them a treat now and then, too. He would apologize to her after school.

The school felt heavier that day, the rupture of routine meal complaints and his mother's worn-out explanation weighing down on him. He sat in his corner, not engaging in the buzz of classmates. An odd quietness cocooned him, his anger reverberating in his clenched fists and tightly pressed lips.

Though he had left in protest and anger, the scent of beans and toast pursued him, a powerful reminder of the bitter reality sandwiched between mundanity and the craving for something more. However, it also whisperingly hinted at the underlying tenacity, the frayed yet unbending spirit, embodied in his mother's patient retort. Sometimes he wished to have inherited her patience.

The day was long, yet the shadows of dawn seemed to linger. The taste of untouched beans and toast, mixed with the flavor of resentment and an unexpected garnish of compassion, consumed him. A brooding day was carved into the annals of his life. He learned much at school, but today, he learned a bit more about life, courtesy of a regular dish of beans and toast served with an unsolicited side of stark reality. Every person has an origin, a beginning, just like Caron. Caron was an average kid with average dreams. His life existed within the four walls of his small house and the classroom where he sat quietly, eyes glued to the chalkboard. But life wasn't easy. His father had abandoned them, leaving him and his mother to wrestle with the financial burdens of everyday living. They were poor but lived with dignity and faith. Which, of course, wasn't made any easier by the number of children his father had left behind. But the struggle in everyday life, peppered with countless children, was nothing compared to the problems he had at school.

In class, Caron had to deal with Terry - the classroom bully. Terry was a big, brawny boy who loved teasing the weaker students, like sharpening his razor on a stone. Caron was his favorite target. Terry couldn't wait to get his hands on Caron.

Terry had cut up several rubber pieces and was throwing them at Caron, mimicking a chant, "What's wrong, Caron?" His voice was coated with mockery, echoing around the near-empty classroom. It was more of an insult than a question. Electric sparks of humiliation and anger sparked in Caron's chest, but he kept his lips sealed. He didn't want to give Terry the satisfaction of his response.

Soon, Terry made a snide remark about Caron's financial situation. He commented that Caron's mother was unable to give him lunch money. That he had the same limp toast with him every day. That jolted Caron. It felt like a personal affront, a malicious jab at his struggle and existence. An uncontrollable rage surged within him. He shot up from his seat, fists clenched, eyes glaring.

His knuckles met Terry's sneering face in a bitter fight. At first, the students stood around, jeering, but their laughter was soon replaced by shock. Caron, the quiet, weak-looking boy, had put up a fight. Eventually, the teacher intervened, and the two boys were separated.

News of the fight reached Terry's parents, and before long, Caron found himself in front of the juvenile court, his heart pounding like a drum. He was sent to a juvenile detention center, a punishment far removed from his quiet life.

Life behind bars was hard. He spent most of the day locked in a small, claustrophobic cell and was allowed out for just a few hours a day. But something good happened in those trapped hours of crushing monotony - Caron discovered his love for basketball.

The sight of an old, worn-out basketball court in the detention center ignited something within him. It was the only source of fun, and Caron found himself drawn to the game like a moth to a flame. He had never played basketball before, but nothing else mattered more than the swish of the net and the feel of the ball against his palms. It became an obsession.

His time playing basketball also gave him the opportunity to demonstrate good behavior. He saw how goals could be made from consistency, precision, and focus. Caron was always the last to leave the court, practicing even in the dim evening light.

His stay in detention ended, along with his obsession. It stayed in him like a pleasant aftertaste. He began training, pushing his body to its limits every day, polishing his raw skills into a refined passion.

Caron's determination didn't go unnoticed. His high school coach observed his evidence and commitment, which soon earned him a spot on the university basketball team. He was a wonder on the court, his humble background only adding to the spectacular narrative of his success. Everyone cheered for the boy out of poverty. Everyone wanted to see him win, see him rise. His family supported him, and his friends celebrated with him.

His incredible performance and sheer dedication grabbed the attention of NBA scouts. Caron was drafted into the professional league in a triumphant turn of events, a testament to his struggles and unbreakable spirit. And he never lost his spirit. He held onto it because, in the end, it was the only thing he could really call his own. Nobody could take that away from him.

Caron's story is not just of an NBA player; it's a tale of an ordinary boy who rose from life's challenges and adversity, guided by hope, resilience and a game of basketball. Every time Caron stepped onto the court, he played not just with a ball but with his past. And in every game, he saw a reflection of his journey - a journey from a bullied boy to an NBA star.

FROM FEAR
TO FEARLESS

"Mental health is as important as physical health. We should all strive for mental wellness just as we do for physical fitness."

-Royce White

Royce sat in the neon-lit classroom, the relentless hum of the fluorescent lights droning in his ears. His pencil danced across the paper, the rhythmic whisper of graphite on the page the only solace in this sterile space. A strange feeling had begun to rise within him; it was like a storm, opaque and threatening, swelling in the pit of his stomach.

Unexpectedly, Royce noticed his breathing becoming shallow, a deep foggy throb seizing his temples. A sense of agitated heat permeated him; droplets of sweat now trickled down his forehead. An uncanny sensation of being watched seared his mind, causing a vehement paranoia to ripple through his body.

This was unfamiliar territory to Royce. He had never felt such an onslaught of uncontrollable dread.

Panic seized him like a vice, leaving him gasping for air and clawing desperately for the grip on normality that was swiftly slipping away. The terror was so overpowering that he couldn't bring himself to raise a hand and request an escape. He felt as though he was drowning in a sea of prying eyes.

Without thinking, he propelled himself from his chair. The empty sound of his desk scraping against the linoleum floor echoed through the classroom, silencing the ongoing discussion. In a blind panic, Royce fled the stifling confinement of the classroom, the door slamming shut behind him. He sunk onto the cold, crimson-brick floor, his labored breaths hanging heavily in the chilled air. He had never experienced anything like this. His heart was beating like loud smoke in his ears, and his hands were shaking as he looked down at them in amazement. He didn't know what happened to him.

Minutes later, the classroom door creaked open, revealing the worried countenance of Ms. Thompson, his English teacher. She knelt beside Royce, her eyes filled with concern as she observed his erratic, shallow breathing.

"Are you alright, Royce?" she asked, her voice a calming balm amidst the chaos of his fears.

A few heavy, panting breaths revealed the state of his crumbling sanity. In the ensuing conversation, Ms. Thompson deduced his peculiar condition: an anxiety attack. Royce didn't understand how this could happen. There was no reason for him to be afraid. He was at school. In safety. Although he was concerned about his grades, there was no reason he should be afraid, which he had told Ms. Thompson.

Imagine your body betraying you, your mind losing control to an invisible foe, and being labeled with a name you had not heard before. Anxiety. The word hung in the air, a dark cloud casting its gloom over Royce's shaken demeanor. Vulnerability was an alien sensation to him, and for the first time, Royce was lost.

And thus began Royce's harrowing journey as he lived with his anxiety. It became his uncontrollable shadow, trailing behind him every day, lurking in the crevices of his mind. Despite his parents' attempts to combat it, shifting him from one high school to another and even a change in colleges, the anxiety followed him like a merciless specter, gnawing at his sanity.

But remember dear reader, anyone's story isn't merely their struggle or fears. It's their strength, resilience, and relentless defiance that they harbor within their hearts to keep going. Such is Royce's tale, too, a tale punctuated with setbacks, colored with worry, yet strengthened by his unyielding courage to confront his anxiety, which continues to unfold with every passing day. In the face of an invisible enemy, Royce stood firm—brave, battered, but never beaten. Royce was a boy of few words, draped in silence like an old, comfortable robe; his world shrank to the confines of school and home. Every day was a loop of the mundane, punctuated only by his privacy and solace. Royce was a portrait of melancholy painted on a summer background of anxiety. His invisible companion was like a let on his shoulders. The seizures are unpredictable and unplanned. In the end, it wasn't the fear that plagued him that bothered him, but the concern that he might have another seizure at an inopportune moment. He was kind hearted and ridiculously intelligent, but anxiety held him back sharply. It weaved around him like a cocoon, trapping him in his comfort zone. It was a war, he was anxious about the world, and at that moment, he was losing. But he had come to terms with that, too.

One day, while making his long and peaceful journey home, he saw a group of uniform-clad children huddled on the basketball court near his apartment. Laughter echoed from the court, a rhapsody played on the keys of camaraderie and joy. Royce was a distant spectator, an uninvited guest on the periphery of their world.

Suddenly, a call rang across the playground. His name. It reached him, shattering the peace like glass on a concrete floor. He shrugged it off as a figment of his hyperactive imagination. Another shout echoed, and this time, Royce swung around. The group was looking at him. Gesturing to him.

"Hey, Royce! Wanna join us for the game?" asked a tall boy, throwing the basketball up and down before throwing it to Royce. He was Frank, the school's star player, his personality as bright as a mid-noon sun.

He and Royce had spoken a few times before. So he was no stranger to him. And yet Royce felt the familiar chill rising inside him. Hands shaking as they wrapped themselves around the ball. The frantic twitching of his eyelids as he studied the ball thoughtfully.

Anxiety flared within Royce, swarming around his consciousness. The twisted irony was it didn't silence him, but it froze him. It was as if he was padded with invisible foam, insulating him from the outside world. Though he desperately tried to carve out the word 'Yes' from his chaotic mind, anxiety had already locked his vocal cords.

Yet, he managed to get through. A faint, almost inaudible whisper emerged. A hard-earned victory.

"Sure." he said, throwing the ball to Frank, who grinned broadly and nodded. It was almost like Frank knew. He looked deep inside Royce and saw the fear that was eating away at him piece by piece. And he had also seen that he fought against it. That he made a conscious decision not to be intimidated by it.

Frank tossed the ball to Royce, his face lit up with a wide smile. As the orange sphere grazed past his palms, he felt a strange tingle, followed by tranquility. A harbinger of change, one he didn't understand yet.

They played together almost every day. At first, Royce wasn't sure if that was a good idea. He wasn't good. Didn't have a talent for it. But the longer they played, the more tricks he learned. It really started to be fun.

Game after game, Royce realized he was playing not just basketball but also with his fears and insecurities. Every time he touched the ball, it seemed to siphon off his anxiety, leaving him lighter and better. Strangely, Royce even enjoyed the feeling of defeat. The camaraderie subdued his fears, his crippling anxiety fading into nothingness.

Every passing day, Royce became a regular fixture on the basketball court. The orange sphere, bouncing rhythmically, matched with his steady heartbeat, a symphony of victory against the clutches of crippling fear.

The day Royce stepped into his once-shattered world as a victor rather than as a victim, a small triumphant smile curled up on his lips. He had conquered his fears. "See ya tomorrow, Royce!" chorused his new friends as they waved goodbye. From then onward, he discovered that his basketball court was not a battlefield but an arena for triumph. His anxiety became a challenge he had faced and overcome rather than a demon haunting his peace. He would use this new strength again and again. He found a new confidence on the court. A new clarity that showed him a path he had not seen before.

So, this is the tale of Royce. A tale of how an anxious, shy boy transformed into a courageous soul who conquered his demons with an orange sphere and a hoop, teaching him not just the rules of basketball but the game of life.

SHOES
CAN FLY

"I can accept failure, everyone fails at something. But I can't accept not trying."

-Michael Jordan

A boy named Michael lived in the vicinity of Brooklyn, New York. The whispers around him were unfavorable and mainly consisted of age-old beliefs about the disadvantages of physical shortcomings. They said, "He's too short; he'll never be a successful basketball player!" Yet Michael clung tenaciously to his dream. Michael Jordan, as the world would later know him, was initially too short to make a lasting impact on the basketball court. This is the tale of that boy who didn't let his height dictate his possibilities and, in the process, became the face of the iconic 'Air Jordans'.

There's an uncommon degree of magic about Michael Jordan. While standing merely 5'11" tall in high school, his heart was as large as a giant's, and his will was indomitable. His audacious dream was to play in the prestigious NBA amidst the likes of physiologically favored athletes who towered well beyond six feet. By society's standard and height-centric perspective, the odds seemed heavily stacked against him.

Undeterred, Michael turned adversity into inspiration. He stepped onto the practice court daily, reminding himself, "The Ceiling is the Roof!" He resolved that nothing in this world would clip his dreams, not even the erroneous dogma of him being too short.

His big break occurred during his time at the University of North Carolina when he noticed an unusual growth spurt. He grew from 5'11" to a considerable 6'6" in a surprisingly short span of time! However, the newfound height did not bolster Michael's arrogance but fuelled his humility. This humility, mixed with heightened ambition, now made him a formidable force on and off the court.

Upon Michael's entry into the NBA, with his extraordinary slam dunks and prowess in handling the ball, he soon became recognized as "His Airness," captivating audiences with his power and grace. With his newly acquired physique and the tricks he had honed through the years, he shattered all previous records and led the Chicago Bulls to six NBA championship wins.

Off the court, Michael garnered significant interest from a slew of brands vying for his endorsement. Among them, the famed sports brand Nike recognized the potential star power in this seemingly unconventional athlete. They trusted their instincts and offered him a deal that would change sports merchandise forever – a pair of sneakers branded in Michael's honor. Thus, the 'Air Jordans' were born.

The Air Jordan shoes hit the market with a bang! They embodied the spirit of Michael Jordan – audacity, skill, agility, and resilience. The Air Jordans were not merely shoes but a symbol of revolution in the world of sports - fostering the notion that height is not a determinant of success but an augmentation of it.

Michael Jordan, the boy who was once considered too short, ascended to unprecedented heights, becoming a legend in the history of basketball. He became the face of 'Air Jordan' not because he grew tall but because he dared to dream tall.

Throughout his career, Michael Jordan debunked the stereotype of height and success in basketball. His tale shows that ambitions aren't enslaved to physical limitations. The trajectory of Michael Jordan's journey sat puny the social construct of height, heralding that success is measured not in feet and inches but in the height and depth of one's passion, determination, and resilience.

"Don't let them call you too short or say you can't make it. Let the world see you rise, and then, let them wear your success on their feet."- Michael Jordan.

FINAL WORD

"Be the best version of yourself in anything you do. You don't have to live anybody else's story."

-Stephen Curry

Like the rest of us, basketball players must endure defeats and setbacks. It's a universal truth in every arena of life: we win some, and then, unavoidably, we lose some, too. We all stumble and face adversities, but how we respond to these challenges defines us, much like in the game of basketball. Sounds familiar, doesn't it?

Every basketball player, irrespective of their skill level, has experienced defeat. It's inevitable. No one can win all the games they play. The critical learning here is that setbacks are essential to progress. Would Michael Jordan have been the player he turned out to be without the painful experience of being left off his high school varsity team?

In basketball, just as in life, you need to fail to learn and get better. The setbacks create learning opportunities. They ignite the passion to improve and perfect. In fact, more often than not, they fuel the journey to greatness.

It doesn't matter if it's fear, injury, or family circumstances that seem to be overwhelming. You always find the real strength within yourself. That is something that no one can take from you. Because at the end of every game, challenge, and situation that seems insurmountable to you, your own strength will bring you to success. Sometimes, it's harder, sometimes easier. Sometimes, it looks like insurmountable hurdles. But if you believe in yourself and work on your skills, you will always emerge victorious.

It doesn't matter what others think of you. It doesn't matter if you have to ask others for help. Asking for help is not a weakness. And trusting others is not forbidden. In the end, like the basketball player, you depend on your team. A team is only as strong as its weakest link.

Just like the basketball players, you shouldn't let yourself be knocked down. Instead, use it as an opportunity to come back stronger. Being resilient doesn't mean that you won't experience difficulty or adversity. It means that you won't allow them to define you or hold you back.

Basketball players are always going to face adversities. Whether it's an injury, a challenging game, or a personal hardship, they had to learn to push through. They teach us to transform our adversities into strength, showing us that struggle is not a stop sign but a stepping stone on the road to success.

To conclude, our failures and setbacks, while disheartening, are crucial stepping stones on the journey to success. They equip us with the lessons needed for personal and professional growth. The struggles, when faced with resilience, can mold us into better individuals.

And who better to learn this life lesson from than the basketball players? The enduring athletes who, when faced with defeat, pick themselves up, dust off, and go once more into the fray, inspiring millions along the way. After all, remember Michael Jordan's mantra, "I've failed over and over and over again in my life, and that is why I succeed."

Made in United States
Troutdale, OR
12/08/2023